FULL EMPLOYMENT
IN YOUR COMMUNITY

THE W. E. UPJOHN INSTITUTE
FOR COMMUNITY RESEARCH

THE INSTITUTE, a privately sponsored nonprofit research organization, was established on July 1, 1945. It is an activity of the W. E. Upjohn Unemployment Trustee Corporation, which was formed in 1932 to administer a fund set aside by the late Dr. W. E. Upjohn for the purpose of carrying on "research into the causes and effects of unemployment and measures for the alleviation of unemployment."

The interest of the Institute in problems of full employment and unemployment is centered at the community level, as distinguished from the national or international level. Its program involves the investigation and evaluation of locally applicable measures for the achievement and maintenance of a high level of employment; the study of the problems of Kalamazoo County with respect to the objective of full employment and with respect to the applicability of various measures for its attainment; and the organization of action programs designed to meet the employment problems of the local community. It is hoped that the experience gained by the Institute and the community in pursuing these objectives will prove helpful to other communities which undertake programs looking toward the attainment of a high level of stable employment.

FULL

EMPLOYMENT

IN YOUR

COMMUNITY

A Report of

THE W. E. UPJOHN INSTITUTE

FOR COMMUNITY RESEARCH

Samuel V. Bennett   Charles C. Gibbons

Hazel S. Cowherd   Harold C. Taylor

Public Administration Service

Chicago : 1947

Preface

I<small>T IS THE PURPOSE</small> of this book to bring together in one place all of the major suggestions that have been made which look toward the achievement and maintenance of full employment, insofar as these proposals relate to action which can be taken at the local level.

This local emphasis does not imply any attempt to deny that many of the problems involved in the achievement and maintenance of a high level of employment are problems which must be solved at the national or even at the international level. It is obvious that the forces which bring about a decline in economic opportunity within a given community, or which subject it to violent change during the ups and downs of the business cycle, are to a considerable extent outside the control of that community.

It is apparent, on the other hand, that the communities of the nation do vary markedly in the extent to which they provide a good standard of living for their citizens and in the extent to which they withstand the alternations of boom and depression. It can hardly be doubted that those communities which attempt to steer their course will ride through the storms of the future more surely than those which fail to take such action.

In recognition of the importance of national effort in the achievement of full employment, nearly all of the books which have been written on the subject deal with national measures. While there is much scattered material related to local programs for full employment, there is no book in which such measures have been brought together so as to be readily accessible to community leaders who may wish to study the problems of their own locality. This volume has been prepared to supply the need for such a book.

It may be of critical importance to the American way of life that we carry out with diligence all of the things that can be done by the individual community, the individual business, and all other groups within the nation to maintain our economy on an even keel. Many people feel that our free enterprise system cannot survive another depression; that when bread lines form, the people will turn, as they did in the last depression, to the central government for aid; and that at the end of that road lies the total loss of individual freedom.

We must make those choices which will tend toward the achievement of a high level of sustained production and employment, or the majority may choose, with however misguided hopes, to relinquish freedom in a desperate search for security. This book suggests some courses of action which free people must take if they hope to achieve continued prosperity within our historic framework of freedom.

The success attained by any given community in providing a fuller and more prosperous life for its citizens will depend ultimately upon the intelligence with which its particular problems are analyzed, and upon the courage and vigor with which those problems are attacked. The authors hope that this book will be useful to those leaders in each community whose efforts may shape its future.

HAROLD C. TAYLOR, *Director*
THE W. E. UPJOHN INSTITUTE
FOR COMMUNITY RESEARCH

ACKNOWLEDGMENTS

This book was read in manuscript by Mr. Walter H. Blucher, Executive Director of the American Society of Planning Officials; Mrs. Rhea M. Eckel, Executive Secretary of the New York State Citizens Council; Dr. Emerson P. Schmidt, Director, Economic Research Department, Chamber of Commerce of the United States; Dr. Louis Wirth, Professor of Sociology, The University of Chicago; and Dr. Theodore O. Yntema, Research Director, Committee for Economic Development. The chapter on "Agriculture and the Problem of Full Employment" was read by Dr. Theodore W. Schultz, Professor of Agricultural Economics, The University of Chicago. Their criticism is gratefully acknowledged, although responsibility for the final draft of the book must rest with the staff of the Institute.

The staff is indebted to Miss Winona M. Lotz, Secretary of the Institute, for assistance in preparing the manuscript for publication and wishes to acknowledge also the assistance of the library staff of Western Michigan College of Education in verifying bibliographical references and writing these references in proper form.

Contents

vii

1

The Community and the
Full Employment Problem

For some time the local community has been losing significance in the minds of those concerned with political, economic, and social affairs. This tendency is evident in the lack of enthusiasm in local elections, in the proneness to forget the local businessman in economic planning, and in the emphasis on national aid in supporting such programs as nursery schools, crime prevention, and old-age assistance. This trend is no doubt due in part to the ease of communication and travel and to the pressure of international ideas. It is well for people to become aware of common problems and goals throughout the world. In emphasizing national and world perspectives, however, one must not lose sight of local opportunities. One must not forget that many problems are local and must be attacked in the local community.

The community as referred to in this book is not limited to any political subdivision. It may cut across several political boundaries. As used in this context the community refers to a geographical area which is bound together by common economic and social ties. A community may be a large city or a suburb. It may be a small town together with the surrounding rural area. In the western states a community may include two or three counties, while on the eastern seaboard it may be only a small section of a county.

In recent years much has been spoken and written concerning the ideals of democracy, free enterprise, and full employment. The community and its relationship to these objectives will be dealt with briefly in these pages.

The Community and Democracy

Outside of the home the ideals of democracy have their first expression in the community. Community institutions such as schools, churches, and playgrounds nurture the ideals of democracy.

Democracy has thrived in America during those periods when community life has been active. The New England town meetings were a significant development because they represented participation by individual citizens in the problems of the community and the nation. They represented the voice of a democratic people. This same technique is being used in our own generation to stimulate people to think and to express opinions on questions of local and national importance. If democracy is to be virile—and it must be virile to survive —it must be strengthened at its roots in the community.

THE COMMUNITY AND FREE ENTERPRISE

Like democracy, the capitalistic system with its components, the price system, the right of private property, the profit motive, free competition, and free enterprise, has been regarded as a characteristically American pattern of life. The right of free enterprise has been especially cherished. For many this is a basic right which must be preserved.

There is a tendency to associate the idea of free enterprise with great industrial organizations like General Motors, U. S. Steel, and duPont. These industries do represent the extent to which free enterprise may be developed. Yet such development is unusual rather than typical. Typical examples of free enterprise are the corner drugstore, the neighborhood grocery, and the hardware store. These businesses are born in the community, are nurtured by the community, and thrive or die in the community. The need for the business, the idea for its establishment, the financing, and the labor come from the local community. Such establishments are an integral part of the community. It would be difficult to find an American community without these evidences of free enterprise.

Even the large industries and businesses are rooted in the community. They receive their initial impetus from the community and wax strong there. Even now it is difficult to divorce many such enterprises from their origin. For example, the Ford Motor Company has plants and representatives in many countries of the world, yet it is still associated with Detroit. Detroit is the community which gave this modern colossus its birth and early support. It is the community to which Ford "belongs."

In the future as in the past, enterprises which will take the places of the obsolescent businesses and industries of today will originate in local communities. There will be fewer failures in communities which know their resources and which can forecast future demands. There will be less waste of financial and human resources in a community which is conscious of the direction of its economic development.

THE COMMUNITY AND THE FULL EMPLOYMENT PROBLEM

Nearly all the material which has been written during the past few years on full employment has been concerned with measures to be taken at the national level. It cannot be denied that these national measures are the ones most likely to influence the level of employment. Booms and depressions appear to be governed by factors largely beyond the control of the local community.

However, it is also evident that national policies and national measures will not insure a high level of employment in any particular community. There are many steps which can be taken in any local community to improve the soundness of its economic base and to increase the opportunity of its own citizens for continuous and productive employment. It is a matter of common observation that communities vary markedly in the extent to which they have been able to offer economic opportunity and stability to their citizens. Many of these differences may have been due to accidental factors of advantage and disadvantage rather than to the diligent efforts of the citizens of the more fortunate communities. There is now, however, an increasing conviction that these important matters must not be left to chance. It is the chief purpose of this book to enumerate as specifically as possible the measures which communities may take to strengthen, expand, and stabilize the local economy.

THE MEANING OF FULL EMPLOYMENT

The real objective of economic activity is obscured by the currently popular slogan "full employment." In order to remove some confusion regarding full employment it will be helpful to indicate first what full employment is not before stating what it is.

Kinds of Unemployment

Full employment does not mean that there will be no unemployment. It must be recognized that a certain amount of unemployment is inevitable in a society where consumers are free to buy what they please and where investors are free to invest or withhold the funds necessary to operate productive establishments.

There are persons in every community who are not employed but who cannot properly be considered as unemployed, for they do not desire to work. This group would include students, housewives, mi-

nors, and the aged. The truly unemployed fall into the following
eight classifications:

Casual Unemployment. Casual unemployment is day-to-day unemployment of short duration. Such unemployment is experienced by
the day worker or by the outdoor worker who cannot work when it
rains.

Seasonal Unemployment. Seasonal changes cause unemployment.
Such unemployment is common on the farm where many workers are
laid off from harvest until spring planting, and it is necessary for them
to find work elsewhere. Some industries, such as food processing, also
experience seasonal fluctuations in activity and in employment.

Labor Reserve Unemployment. Because production is not constant
in most industries and geographical areas, workers are drawn into the
labor force of a community to meet peak production demands. After
the peak is over, they are idle. Such idleness is classified as labor reserve unemployment.

Cyclical Unemployment. The most serious type of unemployment
is that caused by business depression. Businessmen, unable to sell their
products, are forced to lay off workers. Cyclical unemployment is relatively long in duration and substitute work is difficult to obtain during depression periods.

Technological Unemployment. Changes in mechanical processes
and managerial techniques which result in increased productivity of
labor cause labor displacement. This displacement is referred to as
technological unemployment. The added productivity and wealth
resulting from technological improvements may create more jobs in
the long run. However, in a period such as the nineteen-twenties
technological advance may be so rapid and widespread that adjust-
ment of displaced workers may be slow and difficult.

Frictional Unemployment. Frictional unemployment is due to
time lag and labor immobility in the economy. Demand for labor
varies from month to month but labor supply is relatively inelastic;
thus unemployment occurs. Labor may be needed in a particular
locality and workers may be available in another locality. Immobility
of labor is an obstacle to full employment.

Secular Unemployment. It has been thought by some economists
that there are persistent forces at work which tend to reduce opportunity for investment and therefore to reduce production and employment. It is believed that savings tend to increase faster than ways of
making productive use of those savings can be found. These forces
naturally are less evident during boom periods when everything ap-

pears to be going well than during depressions when everything seems to have become disorganized. But if these persistent tendencies do exist, then it means that we shall have a continuous problem of keeping the wheels of our economic machine running fast enough to provide goods and productive employment for everyone. It should be emphasized that not all economists agree that there is any such long-term trend toward unemployment.

Unemployables. In every community there are those who want and need work but who are unable to work because of physical or psychological handicaps.

The Goal of Full Employment

Just as full employment does not mean that there will be no unemployment, it should be clear also that full employment does not mean working more hours, or more days, or more years; or generally working harder than people have been working; or that working should be compulsory. Working hours have been decreasing progressively for many years, and this is in no way considered contrary to the full employment objective. The fact that the goal is not simply the working of more hours is illustrated by a comparison between our world and the world of our grandfathers. In the days when every man tilled his own ground, raised his own food, built his own house, chopped his own firewood, and made his own clothing, it would hardly have occurred to anyone to consider unemployment as a problem. There was plenty of work, but relatively little to show for it.

"Full employment" as used in this book means the opportunity to work for all who are able and willing to work and the maximum utilization of all other factors of production: land, capital, and enterprise. In some respects the expression "full employment" is misleading. The word "full" does not mean what it says, and "employment" as such is not our real objective.

The real goal of full employment is to provide an abundant supply of goods and services for all consumers. It will mean an increased standard of living for all people. Full production without full consumption is a meaningless goal. Production will always be dependent upon purchasing power and the desire to consume.

Full and continuous employment is not simply a pious or humanitarian wish. It is, rather, a goal of utmost importance to the democratic way of life. It is a necessary requirement for freedom or even survival, not only for the individual, but also for democracy. The preservation and expansion of industrial civilization and of the system

of free enterprise are dependent upon our ability to provide every
citizen with the opportunity to contribute to our national wealth and
to share in that wealth.

Socio-economic Interdependence

The following chapters suggest some of the ways in which groups of
citizens organized at the community level can work for full and stable
employment. These measures are not only economic in character, but
social as well. At the local level it is easy to see the interdependence of
social and economic factors. Economic factors predominate perhaps
in the creation of employment opportunities; but social factors directly affect the utilization of existing employment opportunities.

This social and economic interdependence is nowhere more evident
than in the case of housing. A lack of housing can hamper the expansion of industries and interfere with the settling of new industries in
the community.

In deciding whether to locate in a given community, some companies consider not only economic advantages such as a favorable
market, adequate transportation facilities, and a good labor supply,
but also the kind of community in which their employees will live.
They take account of recreational facilities, schools, parks, and hospitals. It is sound business practice and not simply a humanitarian
concern which prompts a consideration of such social and physical
factors. Full employment is a socio-economic problem and the measures which are proposed in this book have this orientation.

PLANNING AT THE COMMUNITY LEVEL

Basically, planning means the capacity to take thought for the
morrow, the capacity to envision distant goals and to direct action
toward the achievement of those goals. Planning is common to all of
us in our individual lives. It is common also in industry. In these
situations, planning is considered desirable. There is a similar contribution which planning can make in the life of a community.
Logically there is no such thing as "no plan"; the decision not to plan
is in itself a plan. We have seen "planlessness" in the lives of individuals, of businesses, in local government, and in national government.

There are at the present time only a few states which do not have
enabling acts for city or county planning. Local planning has become
mandatory for cities over 10,000 population in Massachusetts. In
California, county planning is mandatory. Many states have enabling

legislation for regional planning also. It is to be hoped that the trend toward planning in the local situation may be continued, for it is an important approach to the problem of providing a more prosperous and more secure life for all citizens of the nation.

The planning activities contemplated in these enabling and mandatory acts are theoretically as broad and all-inclusive as the entire social and economic life of the community. In practice, however, the efforts of such official planning groups tend rather naturally to emphasize matters that are ordinarily the functions of local governments. The location of streets, zoning, subdivision control, and provision of municipal services receive more emphasis than industrial stabilization plans, labor-management cooperation, or market analysis.

The theme of this book is not synonymous with community planning in this sense. The focal point in this book is *expansion and stabilization of employment,* community planning being one important aspect of the activities necessary in working toward that objective.

AREAS FOR PLANNING AND ACTION ON EMPLOYMENT PROBLEMS

This book attempts to set forth what has been done and what can be done *at the community level* to maintain a high level of continuous employment. This section is essentially a preview of the book.

One chapter deals with the policies and programs which local government can follow to promote full and stable employment in the community. It is pointed out that as an employer local government directly affects employment opportunity in the community and that as a coordinating agency local government influences indirectly the economic life of the entire community.

Another chapter deals with measures which have been tried in manufacturing companies both to stimulate employment and to provide employment continuity. These proposals represent programs of action which some individual employers are already using and which should be studied carefully by any firm interested in providing more jobs and steadier jobs. Case studies of some companies that have been successful in stabilizing employment are included in a separate chapter.

Proposals are made for expanding and stabilizing employment in business, service occupations, and agriculture. Every type of employer and worker has a stake in achieving and maintaining high levels of employment, production, and consumption.

Workers and organized labor have a responsibility for full employment and a contribution to make toward achieving it. One chapter deals specifically with the ways in which labor can take action toward maintaining a high level of employment. Not only must restrictive practices be eliminated but active steps must be taken to increase productivity.

A survey is given of representative local plans prepared under public or private auspices. Some cities are benefiting from comprehensive plans for economic and social development. The plans of other cities are restricted to programs of public works.

The last chapter in the book gives some suggestions for organizing the citizens of a local community into groups for putting into action the various programs for full and continuous employment. The proposals set forth in this book for industry, labor, agriculture, service occupations, and government are all local in emphasis. These proposals must be implemented by the action of local citizens cooperating to promote their common welfare.

REFERENCES

Beveridge, William H. *Full Employment in a Free Society*. New York: W. W. Norton and Co., 1945. Pp. 429.

Chamber of Commerce of the United States. *Economic Problems of the Post-War; Bibliography, Selected and Annotated*. No. 2. Washington: Chamber of Commerce of the United States, 1944. Pp. 25.

——. Committee on Economic Policy. *A Program for Sustaining Employment*. Washington: Chamber of Commerce of the United States, 1945. Pp. 32.

——. Construction and Civic Development Department. *Bibliography on Postwar Planning*. Washington: Chamber of Commerce of the United States, 1943. Pp. 17.

Committee for Economic Development. *International Trade, Foreign Investment and Domestic Employment Including Bretton Woods Proposals; A Statement on National Policy*. New York: The Committee, 1945. Pp. 26.

——. *A Postwar Federal Tax Plan for High Employment*. New York: The Committee, 1944. Pp. 47.

——. *Toward More Production, More Jobs and More Freedom; A Statement on National Policy*. New York: The Committee, 1945. Pp. 37.

Ezekiel, Mordecai. *Jobs for All through Industrial Expansion*. New York: Alfred A. Knopf, 1939. Pp. 299.

Fitch, Lyle and Horace Taylor. *Planning for Jobs; Proposals Submitted in the Pabst Postwar Employment Awards*. Philadelphia: The Blakiston Co., 1946. Pp. 463.

Gilbert, Milton. "Toward Full Employment," *Fortune*, XXXII (October, 1945), 158–59, 184ff.

Hayek, Friedrich A. *The Road to Serfdom . . . with Foreword by John Chamberlain.* Chicago: University of Chicago Press, 1944. Pp. 248.

International Labour Office. *International Labour Conference, 27th Session, Paris, 1945: The Maintenance of High Levels of Employment during the Period of Industrial Rehabilitation and Reconversion: Second Item on the Agenda.* Report No. 2. Montreal: International Labour Office, 1945. Pp. 181.

Johnston, Eric A. *Steadier Jobs.* Washington: Chamber of Commerce of the United States, 1944. Pp. 13.

Keynes, John Maynard. *The General Theory of Employment, Interest and Money.* New York: Harcourt, Brace & Co., 1936. Pp. 403.

McNair, Malcolm P. "The Full Employment Problem," *Harvard Business Review,* XXIV (1945), 1–21.

National Industrial Conference Board. *Postwar Employment Opportunities; Prepared for the Twenty-eigth Annual Meeting of the Conference Board, May 18, 1944, The Waldorf-Astoria.* New York: National Industrial Conference Board, 1944. Pp. 32.

Pierson, John H. G. *Fiscal Policy for Full Employment.* Occasional Paper No. 45. Washington: National Planning Association, 1945. Pp. 54.

——. *Full Employment and Free Enterprise,* Washington: American Council on Public Affairs, 1947. Pp. 183.

"The Problem of 'Full Employment,' " *American Economic Review,* XXXVI (1946), 280–335. Facts, Issues, and Policies; with discussion by Albert Gailord Hart. Fiscal and Monetary Policy; with discussion by A. R. Sweezy. Wage-Price Policy and Employment; with discussion by Sumner H. Slichter.

Schmidt, Emerson P. *Post-War Readjustments; Bulletins.* Nos. 1–15. Washington: Chamber of Commerce of the United States, 1943–1945.

 1. Why Plan for the Post-War Period? Pp. 13.
 2. Is Post-War Collapse Inevitable: The Short-Run Favorable Factors. Pp. 17.
 3. Some Unfavorable Factors. Pp. 22.
 4. Maladjustments in the Post-War. Pp. 21.
 5. Absorbing the Total Labor Supply. Pp. 30.
 6. The Problem of Business Incentives. Pp. 38.
 7. Small Business: Its Place and Problems. Pp. 36.
 8. Deficit Spending and Private Enterprise. Pp. 41.
 9. Full Employment: Its Politics and Economics. Pp. 24.
10. Inflation and the Post-War. Pp. 22.
11. Freedom and the Free Market Inseparable. Pp. 11.
12. Economic Policy: Means and Ends. Pp. 21.
13. Can Government Guarantee Full Employment? Pp. 26.
14. Maintaining Purchasing Power in the Transition. Pp. 18.
15. Mitigating Depressions: Some Suggestions for Policy. Pp. 29.

Slichter, Sumner. "More Job Givers Wanted," *Fortune,* XXXII (October, 1945), 160–61, 190ff.

Stead, William H. *Democracy against Unemployment: An Analysis of the Major Problems of Post-War Planning.* New York: Harper & Brothers, 1942. Pp. 280.

Swanson, Ernst W. and Emerson P. Schmidt. *Economic Stagnation or Progress; A Critique of Recent Doctrines on the Mature Economy, Oversavings, and Deficit Spending.* New York: McGraw-Hill Book Co., 1946. Pp. 212.

Twentieth Century Fund. *Postwar Planning in the United States; An Organization Directory.* Organization Directory No. 2. New York: The Fund, 1943. Pp. 96.

United States Congress. Senate. Committee on Banking and Currency. *Bibliography on Full Employment.* (79th Congress, 1st Session, Senate Committee Print No. 2.) Washington: Government Printing Office, 1945. Pp. 56.

Wallace, Henry A. *Sixty Million Jobs.* New York: Reynal & Hitchcock, Simon & Schuster, 1945. Pp. 216.

Wootton, Barbara. *Freedom under Planning.* Chapel Hill: University of North Carolina Press, 1945. Pp. 180.

2

Local Government Measures to Promote Full Employment

T HERE are three broad ways in which local government can make a contribution toward the achievement of a high and stable level of employment:

1. By providing a suitable environment or "climate" for economic and social development.

2. By taking measures to stabilize public employment and to co-ordinate it with the total employment need in the community.

3. By promoting the economic expansion of the community in co-operation with other groups in the community.

THE COMMUNITY CLIMATE

The stability of a community's economic structure is affected by the kind of "climate" which prevails in the community. Is it a good community in which to live? Is it a good community in which to work? Does it offer prospects for sound and continuous economic and social development? What do visitors think of the community? Do industries seek to locate in the community? Some of the ways in which local government can improve the climate are given below.

Tax on Real and Personal Property

The taxes on real and personal property are factors which affect the community climate. Generally speaking, high taxes discourage home ownership and industrial development.

A high tax rate in one community may be necessary because property valuations are low. A low tax rate may be possible in another community because property valuations for purposes of taxation are close to the market value of the property. A comparison of the costs of living or of operating a business in two cities should obviously not be made on the basis of tax rate alone.

While the estimated tax load usually gives a better basis for comparison than tax rate, the tax problem should be studied further in terms of what the tax dollar buys in each community. The kinds of services and the efficiency with which those services are rendered are important considerations in this connection. For example, in city "A" there may be no municipal garbage collection service, or, assuming there is, collections may be made once a week rather than twice a week as in city "B."

It is in these terms that the tax rate must be evaluated in comparing cities. In these ways taxes encourage or discourage home ownership and the location of new industry in the community and stimulate or retard the social and economic development of the community.

Zoning Ordinances

The general purpose of a zoning ordinance is to promote the public health, morals, safety, and prosperity of the community. A community without a zoning ordinance faces the risk of having a business or industrial organization locate in or near an area which is chiefly residential. Homeowners in the area may find that their homes will depreciate in value. One reason for having zoning ordinances is to prevent incompatible uses of land and the subsequent decline of an area.

Zoning ordinances serve other purposes, however, in addition to preventing blight and protecting the interests of parties directly concerned. These ordinances should make adequate provisions for the business and industrial needs of the community and thereby promote the interests of homeowners and other persons in the community. The physical and social advantages of a community are to a large extent made possible by the presence of industries in the community. The expansion of present industry and the development and location of new industries are dependent on a supply of suitable sites zoned for industrial use. This provision for industrial development is as important as preventing the intermixture of residences and industrial plants.

Zoning ordinances need to be reviewed from time to time to see whether they are serving the economic as well as the social interests of the community.

Facilities and Services

It is idle to think in terms of attracting more industries and more people to the community if the needs of the people or of industries now in the community are inadequately served. The minimum requirements include adequate housing facilities, school plants, recreational facilities, parking facilities, local transportation service, hospitals, street lighting, water supply, gas and electricity, sewage disposal, and police and fire protection.

Because the bearing of these public services on the achievement of full and stable employment is rather indirect they are not discussed in detail. It must not be overlooked, however, that the long-run attractiveness of the community as a place in which to live and work is influenced by the extent to which these services are adequately provided at a reasonable cost.

Social Environment

Community climate depends in part on social conditions. Educational opportunities, the frequency and types of crime, the extent of delinquency, the prevalence of slums, and the state of public health are some of the social factors which determine the climate of a community.

The problems listed here are not isolated, and they cannot be effectively attacked in isolation. The problem of delinquency may be associated with the presence of slum areas or the absence of adequate recreational facilities, which, in turn, may result from the lack of sound zoning provisions. An effective attack upon these problems can be made only after many of the basic facts about a community are known and the interrelationships of these facts are observed.

MEASURES TO STABILIZE EMPLOYMENT

Two Rivers, Wisconsin, affords an example of the benefits of adopting employment stabilization procedures. An annual wage was substituted for an hourly wage. A flexible work week was established, and employees were trained so that they could be transferred from one department to another. Thus, street sweepers work 30 hours each week in the winter and 50 hours in the summer. The park superintendent is manager of the ice skating rinks in the winter, and other employees are shifted in a similar manner.

The results have been significant. Work stretching no longer occurs. In four years of operation of the plan no regular employee has been laid off. Furthermore, no employee has had to seek public relief. Finally, since the employment stabilization policy was put into effect, no employee has become involved in a lawsuit because of a delinquent account.

As an employer, the local government can take steps which directly affect the stability of employment through the public works program, the educational system, and the purchasing policies of local government units.

Public Works

The main purpose of a public works program is to furnish facilities for better services to the community. The need for services, and not employment, is the ultimate justification for public works.

While the purpose of a public works program is not to maintain or to raise the level of employment in a community, the planning of such a program on a long-term basis influences the level of employment, in addition to providing for necessary and orderly changes in the physical environment. Some of the advantages of long-range planning may be summarized as follows:[1]

1. By advance planning the aggregate of public expenditures can better be held within the financial means of the community, provide a surplus of borrowing power available for emergencies, and thus insure unimpaired credit.

2. Long-term planning tends to keep the tax rate even from year to year by avoiding wide variations in expenditure.

3. By cutting down wide annual fluctuations in public expenditures, advance planning tends to be a factor in stabilizing economic conditions in a city. As such it makes possible adequate and economical planning by real estate agencies, the construction industry, utility companies, etc., all of which depend upon foreknowledge of conditions for their successful operation.

4. With plans in readiness for prompt execution it is possible to utilize public works for relief of unemployment during periods of depression and for cutting down the seasonal fluctuation of employment in the construction industry.

5. Careful planning of a city's expansion on the basis of study of past trends and probable future needs tends to save unnecessary expenditures.

All public works programs should be planned well in advance—for five to ten years, or even longer. Some of the projects in the program will have to be carried out without delay; others will be postponable. Those projects which are postponable may be carried out during periods of low economic activity when they will provide needed employment. In the final analysis these programs must be evaluated in terms of their contribution to the convenience and prosperity of persons in the community.

[1]United States Department of Commerce, *Advance Planning of Public Works in the District of Columbia* (Washington: Government Printing Office, 1933).

Education

Many proposals have been advanced to improve the public school system from the standpoint of more adequately relating educational and vocational training to the economic needs and employment opportunities in the community.

Vocational Guidance and Training. A program of vocational guidance and training for students who do not expect to go to college should be influenced by the characteristics of the community. Such a program needs orientation in terms of the present economic structure of the community, its industrial growth, population forecast for the next two decades, and occupational opportunities in the nation as well as in the community. Vocational guidance and training must be developed in terms of the interests, aptitudes, and expectations of the students served. Neither the individual student nor the community is served well if a program of vocational guidance and training lacks a broad community orientation.

Apprenticeship Training. A program of study and work experiences in the crafts or trades under the supervision of the local school board and in cooperation with industry and labor organizations merits consideration. Such a program could be included as part of the four-year high school course or might be undertaken for one or two years following graduation. It would give the student a better orientation toward a vocation and a better appreciation of related academic work, and it would provide industry with a more adequate supply of skilled labor.

Opportunities for the Handicapped. Local school officials can reduce the number of unemployed by providing training for handicapped students. Experience with handicapped workers in industry has shown that a handicapped person, properly placed and trained, is a better-than-average worker. An attempt by school officials to train handicapped pupils for jobs which they can do will not only conserve and utilize the human resources of the community, but will also be a preventive step against problems which arise among a group of "unemployables."

Purchasing Policy

Some companies have helped to stabilize employment by improving their purchasing procedures. For example, the policy followed by one seasonal manufacturer producing sports equipment is to order supplies for a period of one year but to have deliveries spaced over the fifty-two weeks. Not only is he able to make the best use of his warehousing facilities, but he also makes it possible for the producer of raw materials to arrange his work schedule more efficiently.

While the situation in local government varies in many respects from that found in industry, regularizing the purchase of equipment and supplies for governmental departments would have a stabilizing influence on the manufacturers of finished products and the producers of raw material.

At the present time the opposite policy generally prevails. "Our purchasing practices are organized to have all supplies purchased and delivered by September 15 so as to release the time of our business manager for other duties during the school session."[2] Spacing deliveries, while involving additional responsibilities for the business manager, may have consequences which will justify the additional work.

The effect of a school's purchasing policy on the stability of public and private employment has not been of concern in the past to educational administrators or to municipal government officials. Since policies of municipal purchasing and financing may have effects on the economic life of the community, local government, just as much as business and the national government, has an obligation to consider the long-range effects of its purchasing policies.

EXPANDING THE LOCAL ECONOMY

The question of whether a community should expand industrially and in what specific ways is important to the community as a whole—to citizens, local government, and existing businesses and industries as well as to prospective businesses and industries which may consider locating in the community. A sound answer to this question must have as its basis a factual study of the economic structure of the community, including its resources and its needs. In most communities a factual study can best be undertaken by the planning commission or by the municipal research bureau, which already have research facilities. If, after a careful study of its economic structure, responsible officials in the community agree that expansion along industrial and business lines is desirable and feasible, a sound program can then be mapped out.

Several aspects of this problem will be considered briefly in this section: the question of responsibility for the development of a program of business and industrial expansion; the orientation or objectives of such a program; the study of the community's resources as a

[2]*The School Executive*, LXIV, No. 8 (April, 1945), p. 68.

prerequisite to the development of a program for business and industrial expansion; and the basis for selecting industrial prospects. A more detailed consideration of some of these topics will be found in the United States Department of Commerce publications listed among the references at the end of this chapter.

Responsibility for Programs of Expansion

While programs for business and industrial expansion have in the past been initiated and developed principally by special groups in the community, it has become evident that the soundness of such programs affects the welfare of all persons in the community. For this reason local government should participate in the development of programs for industrial expansion. First of all, government represents the citizens of the community who are not otherwise represented in the effort to strengthen or expand the economic base of the community. Secondly, local government can serve as a coordinating agency for the various public and private groups which are actively engaged in efforts to promote business and industrial development—agencies such as the real estate board, the chamber of commerce, transportation companies, and trade associations. Finally, local government, perhaps through its planning commission or its research bureau or in cooperation with other organized bodies, can undertake the factual studies necessary to arrive at answers to such questions as: What businesses and industries does this community need? What kind can it attract? What particular companies should it solicit?

The participation of local governments in programs for business and industrial development is advocated for practical reasons. The surveys and studies cannot be undertaken by a single company or by a group of companies. Existing businesses and industries may have no personal reason for undertaking these surveys and studies. Even if they have, they are not in as favorable a position as is some branch of local government to collect and interpret the essential data about the community. To some extent research may already be a function of certain city officials.

The Objectives

In the past, most towns and cities developed and promoted programs for business and industrial expansion on the assumption that more businesses and more industries meant more prosperity for these communities. This belief has not always been justified. In some cases the pursuit of this policy has resulted in weakening the economic structure of the community and has been followed by undesirable social consequences.

Although the specific objectives of a program of industrial expansion will be different in each community, the general objectives will be:

1. To achieve a balanced economic structure.
2. To reduce seasonal and cyclical fluctuations in employment.
3. To provide opportunities for a high level of employment for all persons in the labor force.
4. To increase the standard of living through a high level of production and consumption.

Study of Resources for Industrial Development

A study of the community's resources is the first step in determining what industries can operate profitably in the community and can contribute to the economic and social welfare of the community. This study should be made in terms of the factors which a company might consider in evaluating a community for a plant location.

The features of a community which are basic to industries are: materials for production, labor supply, industrial sites, electrical power, water, industrial fuel, transportation facilities, proximity to markets, distribution facilities, living conditions, existing laws and legal trends which are of significance to prospective industries, the tax structure of a community, and its physical climate.

The relative importance of these factors varies from one industry to another. In the case of a baker, for example, the materials for production need not be found in the community in which he locates. For him, however, proximity to markets is a primary consideration. On the other hand, the relative importance of these two factors is reversed in the case of the manufacturer of furniture.

With regard to these basic factors, the pattern of strengths and weaknesses differs from one community to another. Each of these factors should be appraised and checked against the requirements of different industries in order to have a basis for selective rather than indiscriminate solicitation of business and industrial prospects. A United States Department of Commerce publication, by Frederic W. Olmstead, entitled *Basic Industrial Location Factors* gives in some detail the kinds of information which are useful in appraising each of these factors and also gives an evaluation of the importance of each factor in various industries.

As a further aid in the selection of industrial prospects or in expanding existing industrial facilities a research organization in the community can consider products that are used in the community but which are being produced elsewhere. Perhaps technical advice may be necessary in answering questions such as: Which of these products can be produced in this community and sold at a competitive price?

While the most important function of the research organization is to give a factual basis to programs for industrial expansion, it may be feasible and desirable for it to serve the economic interests of the community in several other ways. For example, existing local industries might be studied to determine their long-run strengths and weaknesses. If some of the important local industries are declining, it is important for the community to know this in time to take some steps toward getting new industries.

Sometimes the study of local industry will reveal related industries that might be encouraged to locate in the community. Companies in other cities which supply products for local industries might find it convenient to have a plant in the community, or subcontractors may be attracted to the community.

Many companies do not have the resources and the staff necessary to study the field of foreign exports. In some cases, a substantial volume of business may be derived from this source. Again, the research organization can most efficiently make the survey of export possibilities for industries of the community.

Selecting Industrial Prospects

In determining whether a particular company should be encouraged to locate in a community, the sponsors of the development program should be guided not only by the development which they believe to be desirable for the community but also by the company's chances for successful operation in the community. Following are some of the questions which should be answered in determining whether a particular prospect is likely to be successful and also is likely to be an asset to the community:

1. Are the general management policies progressive and conducive to the general betterment of the community and its people?

2. Are the personnel policies of the company satisfactory and its wage scale above average?

3. Is the business run so as to minimize seasonal fluctuations in employment?

4. What is the competitive situation in the industry in which the

company operates? It is difficult for a company that has to meet cut-throat competition to be a good member of the community.

    5. What are the potential sales and payroll of the company?

    6. What marketing area will be served from the city?

In the preparation and development of a program for industrial development, it is necessary for communities to study their own resources and the prospective companies with the same care and thoroughness with which the companies investigate the community. Local government should participate in factual studies of the community and in the other phases of the program.

REFERENCES

Chicago Plan Commission. *Annual Report, 1944.* Chicago: The Commission, 1944. 36 unnumbered pp.

Future Springfield, Inc. *Research in Action.* Springfield, Mass.: Future Springfield, Inc., 1946. 28 unnumbered pp.

Logsdon, C. S. *A Guide for Local Industrial Promotion.* U. S. Bureau of Foreign and Domestic Commerce, Economic (Small Business) Series No. 47. Washington: Government Printing Office, 1946. Pp. 29. First issued in 1945 in processed form.

Lohmann, Karl B. *Principles of City Planning.* New York: McGraw-Hill Book Co., 1931. Pp. 395.

National Association of Housing Officials. Committee on Community Relations in Housing Developments. *Community Relations in Urban Low-Rent Housing; First Report.* Publication No. N123. Chicago: The Association, 1940. Pp. 19.

New England Town Planning Association. *Community Planning for Younger Citizens; A Manual for Teachers.* Boston: The Association, n.d. Pp. 32.

New Haven Chamber of Commerce. Housing Committee. *Housing and Construction in the New Haven Area; Study and Recommendations.* New Haven: New Haven Chamber of Commerce, 1945. Pp. 56.

Olmstead, Frederic W. *Basic Industrial Location Factors; Guide for Evaluating an Area's Resources for Industrial Development.* Washington: U. S. Department of Commerce, Office of Small Business, Area Development Division, n.d. Pp. 10. Processed.

Segoe, Ladislas et al. *Local Planning Administration.* Chicago: International City Managers' Association, 1941. Pp. 699.

3

Expanding and Stabilizing Industrial Employment

A Responsibility and an Opportunity

THE MAJOR RESPONSIBILITY for maintaining high levels of employment is often placed on industry. It should be recognized in this connection that manufacturing has consistently provided not more than 25 per cent of peacetime jobs. Trade and service occupations, including construction work, on the other hand, accounted for more than 50 per cent of nongovernment employment in 1940.

Industry is undoubtedly more important as a source of jobs, however, than the number of people employed would indicate. The earnings of industrial workers provide the basis for many other kinds of economic activities, since many businesses and trades are supported largely by the earnings of industrial people. Taxes paid by industry and by industrial workers support a large number of the workers in government service.

It must be recognized that the goal of the individual manufacturer is not a large number of workers on his payroll but rather a high level of production which will produce a satisfactory profit on the investment. High levels of production benefit workers also by making possible increases in the standard of living. Although high levels of production and high levels of employment usually go together, it should be clear that the real goal of any economic system must be high levels of production. It would be economically disastrous if all manufacturers were to confuse the goal of full employment with the goal of full production as one paper manufacturer did when he reduced the speed of the paper machines 20 per cent in order to spread available work during slack periods.

Motivation for Employment Stabilization

It seems clear that the country will benefit economically and socially to the extent that it is possible to stabilize employment at a high level. The real problem is whether the managements of various companies believe that the benefits of stabilized employment are sufficient to offset the cost.

Employers contemplating action to stabilize employment should consider which of the factors listed below will operate to compensate the company for the effort and cost put into a stabilization program:

1. Perhaps the most direct benefit to the company from an employment stabilization program will be a reduction in the amount of unemployment compensation tax paid. Practically all states now have provisions for experience rating in their unemployment compensation tax laws. Geo. A. Hormel & Company estimates that it is saving $27.00 per $1,000 of payroll in unemployment compensation taxes because of its success in stabilizing employment. The stabilization program of the Geuder, Paeschke and Frey Company of Milwaukee reduced the company's unemployment compensation payments from an estimated $33,500 (if the law had been in effect in 1934) to $30.60 actually paid during the first seven months after the law became effective on July 1, 1936. Many other companies report savings of equal size from this source.

2. Regular production means that the manufacturer will have to pay less money in overtime payments during periods of peak production.

3. High tax rates on corporation income also have a bearing on employment stabilization. A stable operation will produce greater profit because the high tax rate prevents a company from building up large reserves during good times to carry it over periods of slack business.

4. Curtailed operations are more serious than they once were because of the high "break-even point" which prevails in most manufacturing industries today. Manufacturers start to lose money sooner when business declines.

5. Steady production results in lower costs per unit because a larger volume of goods can be manufactured with no additional charges for machinery, floor space, interest, obsolescence, rent, insurance, property taxes, and indirect labor.

6. Regular production prevents labor turnover, which is expensive. Competent employees will stay with a company which provides them stable employment. If employment is subject to frequent interruptions, employees lose their skill and enthusiasm, and new employees have to be hired to fill the places of experienced employees who found

jobs in more stable companies. Even after costly training, the new employees produce goods lower in quality and quantity than experienced employees produce. Many companies have reported fewer accidents and appreciable savings in workmen's compensation costs since regularized operations have reduced the number of new workers on the payroll.

7. A company benefits in many ways from the large amount of planning in production and distribution which must precede any program for stabilized employment. For example, planned production often permits longer machine runs, which produce higher quality goods and lower unit cost.

8. A company often benefits in terms of greater loyalty and cooperation from workers as a result of the efforts to provide them with stable employment. Workers who feel secure in their jobs will be less resistant to technological changes. As a result of stabilized employment, a company often derives some goodwill from customers and other members of the community.

Seasonal and Cyclical Stabilization

Most employment stabilization techniques are directed toward the elimination of seasonal fluctuations in employment. Cyclical trends have usually been considered to be beyond the control of any one company. Reducing seasonal and cyclical fluctuations in sales, production, and employment is really one process from the standpoint of a given company. A company can provide jobs for people only as long as it is able to meet competition. In order to be in a good competitive position during a depression or at any other time, a company must have efficient procedures for production and distribution. The reduction of seasonal fluctuations in employment has been shown to result in reduced production costs; reduced costs, in turn, help the company to expand its sales and to provide work during periods of business depression.

Insofar as measures to stabilize employment over short periods of time are effective in raising and stabilizing purchasing power, they inevitably have a beneficial effect in warding off depressions. It has been pointed out that depressions often seem to be initiated by relatively small disturbances of some particular area of the economy that spread and multiply to bring about general depression conditions.

The question often arises as to what one company can do to prevent or combat a depression aside from keeping itself in a competitive position so that it can reach adequate markets. It has been proposed that a company can make some contribution by adopting a fairly uniform rate of investment and production from year to year rather than by letting its investment and production follow the general trend of business. The case for and against the pursuance of a contra-cyclical investment policy on the part of an individual company has been summarized by Emerson P. Schmidt in the quotation given below:[1]

Strong, growing and well-established business units should experiment with the possibility in their investment and expansion policies of ignoring, in whole or in part, threatening unemployment. If a substantial number of industries would maintain a fairly uniform rate of investment from year to year, including maintenance and replacement, this, in itself, would help to place a cushion under depression. This may be regarded as dangerous. But if all businesses drastically cut the outlays for replacements, new equipment and plant, this is also dangerous, both in terms of the bankruptcy rate and in terms of the political counterforces which extreme contraction generates, as in the 1930's both here and in Europe. By avoiding overexpansion when others are expanding in response to a mere speculative boom, the long-run basis for steady expansion is more thoroughly grounded.

By following a policy contrary to this suggestion, businessmen install their capital at the highest possible prices. By concentrating so much expansion during the boom and especially the later stages of the boom, when prices are the highest, and failing to construct new capital during depressions, industry tends to become loaded with high priced capital. It is in the interest of the individual business unit, as well as the general interest, to reverse this irra-tional process of capital formation.

This should be enough incentive to encourage some reversal of the poli-cies of the past. To be sure, there are some handicaps in postponing capital formation when it appears to be desperately needed and some dangers in capital construction during depressions when future demands are uncertain. But certainly the past policies following an opposite contour have also been fraught with danger, as recent history so well demonstrates. As a guide for the suggestions made herein, business management may readily recognize that the longer a boom has continued, the greater are the statistical prob-abilities that it will terminate soon; the longer the depression has continued the greater the probabilities that it will be transformed into recovery. This rough guide, closely analyzed, may do something to postpone ill-advised ex-pansion and to encourage the resumption of new capital building before boom conditions set in.

It should be emphasized in connection with the contracyclical in-vestment and production policies just proposed that it is suggested that they be carried out by individual business enterprises on a volun-tary basis. It is obvious that if the management of all concerns in a

[1]Emerson P. Schmidt, *Mitigating Depressions* (Washington: Chamber of Com-merce of the United States, 1945), pp. 11–12.

specified industry were to get together and agree on expansion policies and producton levels, such action would be a violation of the
spirit of free competition and of laws against monopolistic practices.

It is recognized that for a given company to carry out such policies
by itself presents a very serious problem. The management of that
particular enterprise may feel certain that if the entire industry goes
full blast for a few years, the industry will inevitably reach that point
of saturation which will usher in a depression. However, they cannot
have any assurance whatsoever that their own pursuance of a contracyclical policy will have any effect upon that undesired outcome. If
their competitors continue to make hay while the sun shines, then
the business which follows a contracyclical policy will simply wind
up by doing less business for itself without having helped in any way
to mitigate the force of the anticipated depression. It is admittedly
difficult to see what motivation there is for an individual enterprise
to attempt to stave off forces which are so largely beyond its control.
However, the contracyclical measures which have been discussed have
been proposed seriously; and if a way can be found to make them
effective, the possible beneficial results are great.

The remainder of this chapter deals with a large number of proposals which have been made for reducing cyclical as well as seasonal
fluctuations in employment. No attempt has been made to consider
every aspect of industrial operation in this light. Financial management of a company, for example, is not discussed. The methods proposed for expanding and stabilizing employment are discussed under
four headings: planning for production efficiency, product development, sales program, and personnel procedures.

PLANNING FOR PRODUCTION EFFICIENCY

In order to produce goods at a price that will result in maximum
sales and maximum employment, a company must have efficient production. As one part of planning for full employment, the management of each company should study and improve plant layout and
equipment, management and personnel policies and procedures, and
production techniques and processes. Every economy consistent with
sound operation should be made because these economies will result
in decreased cost and decreased selling prices, which, in turn, will
result in more sales and more jobs for employees. One ingredient of
a successful program for employment stabilization is an accurate
analysis of the production process. It will be helpful, for example,
to know the number of man-hours required to produce a unit of

product. Adequate records must be kept regarding production costs and inventories. Time studies, job evaluations, and other phases of industrial engineering will make their contributions to more efficient production processes.

Producing Articles for Stock

The most common method used for maintaining steady employment is the production of articles for stock. This method is useful in reducing seasonal rather than cyclical fluctuations in employment. When the National Industrial Conference Board undertook a study of stabilization methods in 1940, 130 of the 203 companies contacted reported that they used manufacture for stock as a stabilization method.[2] The idea of producing articles during slack seasons for sale during seasons of better business is simple. The administration of such a plan is often quite complex, however, and consideration must be given to the following points:

1. Durability of the product. Before producing large quantities of material for stock one must be certain that the goods will not deteriorate during storage.

2. Obsolescence. One must consider whether design and style changes during the storage period will decrease the value of the product. Production of goods for stock is much more feasible if the products are well standardized. Companies handicapped by frequent style changes in their merchandise may be able to manufacture certain staple articles for stock without too much risk. The Hickey-Freeman Company, for example, produces conservative black and brown overcoats during slack seasons.

3. Storage costs. The question always arises as to whether existing storage facilities are adequate or whether additional warehouses will have to be built or rented. The value of the product per unit of space required to store it is an important consideration in deciding whether it will be profitable to produce articles for storage. The cost of handling the goods is often a large part of the total cost of storing a product. Sometimes customers can be persuaded to accept advance shipments when the manufacturer's warehouses are full.

4. Price changes during storage. Consideration must be given to the possibility that the price of the stored product will drop appreciably during the storage period. If the manufacturer is a major producer, the very fact that he has large quantities of goods stored may

[2]F. Beatrice Brower, *Reducing Fluctuations in Employment* (New York: National Industrial Conference Board, 1940).

have an unfavorable effect on the price. If the product is stored for several months, general business conditions may change enough to necessitate a change in price. In all cases it is wise to set a maximum on the size of inventory to be accumulated through production for stock.

5. Capital tied up. Another consideration in the production of goods for stock and storage is the amount of capital tied up during the storage period. The large amount of capital required to produce goods for stock is one of the principal factors preventing the steel industry from producing goods for stock. Even if the company finds it possible and advisable to make this capital outlay, the interest on the increased investment must be recognized as a business expense.

Richard R. Deupree, president of the Procter and Gamble Company, points out[3] that many manufacturers can stabilize their production and employment by producing goods at the rate at which the goods are consumed. Mr. Deupree expresses the belief that 85 per cent of the goods in this country are consumed evenly. Much unstable employment arises from the fact that these goods are not purchased evenly. For eighty years the Procter and Gamble Company had wide fluctuations in employment while they tried to produce to the buying curve. By planning their production around the consumption of goods rather than around the buying of goods, since 1923 the company has been able to guarantee a worker forty-eight weeks of work in the calendar year, provided he wants to work and will take any job that is available.

Timing of Design Changes

After a company has become conscious of the benefits of stabilizing employment, some improvements may be made in the timing of design changes. It may be desirable to introduce new models at a time that otherwise would be a slack period. Until 1930 most automobile manufacturers spaced their models throughout the year. Then the Ford Motor Company introduced yearly models in January and thereby increased seasonal fluctuations in sales and employment. There was an employment peak in the spring and early summer and a sharp decline in employment in October and November. In 1934 manufacturers agreed to introduce models in the late fall. This action shifted the slack season to late summer and early fall

[3]Richard R. Deupree, "Management's Responsibility toward Stabilized Employment," in *Management Planning for Employment Stabilization* (New York: American Management Association, 1945).

when other jobs are easier to get and the living expenses of workers are not so high.

At a time when most radio manufacturers introduced new models twice a year, the Radio Corporation of America started introducing new models whenever sales showed signs of slackening. This practice was effective in reducing fluctuations in employment. Such a practice requires fast action in designing, manufacturing, and distributing new models.

Steady Purchases

If a company will make an effort to maintain a steady flow of incoming parts and materials, this will have some effect on the stabilization of employment for that company as well as for its suppliers. Receiving incoming parts and materials as needed decreases fluctuations of employment in the receiving and warehouse departments. In some companies goods must be processed within a certain length of time after receipt. McCormick and Company, Inc., packer of teas and spices, which has an enviable record in stabilizing employment, has used planning and control of purchasing to stabilize employment. The Procter and Gamble Company finds an additional advantage in regularizing purchases: it can often secure lower prices by buying its materials on an annual basis. The materials are then shipped at regular intervals to meet the production needs of the company.

Scheduling Maintenance Work

Forty-four of the 203 companies included in the Conference Board study of employment stabilization reported that they used the scheduling of maintenance work as a stabilization method. Seventy-five of the 247 firms interviewed in a survey of Wisconsin employers reported the use of deferred work to stabilize employment. Cyclical as well as seasonal fluctuations in employment may be reduced by doing only necessary inspection and repair of equipment during boom periods, saving the major rebuilding, retooling, and overhauling of equipment and plant for periods of slack business.

A company can reduce fluctuations in employment by putting maintenance workers on production jobs during peak periods and by transferring production workers to maintenance jobs during slack periods. A company can even have the construction and maintenance work needed during a period of peak production handled by a contractor. This method avoids the necessity of hiring workers for the construction job and then laying them off after the job is finished. A contractor has a better opportunity to provide steady work for construction workers.

The Warner and Swazey Company has taken advantage of the practice of doing maintenance work during periods of low production by soliciting its customers for orders to rebuild lathes during these slack periods. This reconditioning can only be done when the equipment is not in use. By this method Warner and Swazey has made a considerable contribution toward stabilizing income for its workers.

Packaging

The packaging of many manufactured products affects the volume of sales and also the seasonal fluctuations in sales. An efficient package can reduce production costs by saving labor and preventing spoilage. Sales are increased by packaging which protects the product and, if possible, displays it. Little macaroni was sold in the summertime until after it was put into airtight packages which protect it from moisture and insects. Sanitary and attractive packages for candy, cookies, milk, ice cream, and cheese have increased and stabilized the sales of these products. By reducing packaging costs and increasing sales appeal, the proper package makes possible higher levels of sales, production, and employment.

Cost Reduction

It is important to the workers of a company as well as to the management for the company to be able to compete favorably from the standpoint of the price of its products. In periods of declining demand, the first manufacturer to feel the shock is the one with the highest prices if other factors are equal. In this way, unemployment comes first to employees in companies with high production costs. Whenever sound economies result in lower selling prices for products, more customers are able to purchase the product. It is quite possible that cost reduction is the most effective single method of achieving a high level of continuous employment.

For their own welfare, workers should cooperate with management in sound programs of cost reduction. Management, on the other hand, has the responsibility for making cost reductions that will be to the best interests of customers, workers, and owners of the business.

Analyzing and Simplifying Jobs

A program of job analysis and job simplification will make a contribution to employment stabilization by increasing efficiencies and by making more feasible the transfer of workers from one job to another. The requirements of each job must be known before it is possible to develop standards for hiring and placing employees.

PRODUCT DEVELOPMENT

From the standpoint of reducing seasonal fluctuations in employment, increasing the general level of production and employment in the company, and guarding against a severe slump in business during a depression, one of the effective methods a company can use is to sponsor a continuous program of product development so that its products will effectively meet the customers' demands with respect to both quality and price. Experience has shown, moreover, that some products are more nearly "depression proof" than others.

Diversification or Dovetailing of Products

Often a company can both expand and stabilize its employment level by diversifying its line of products. One-fourth of the companies covered in the Conference Board survey developed new products or models as part of their employment stabilization programs. The primary objective is to find a secondary or fill-in product that may be produced during the slack seasons of the main product. In order for dovetailing to be successful, the period of maximum activity of the new commodity must coincide roughly with the period of minimum activity of the commodities normally produced. In some cases where the secondary product is not seasonal, it may still be made seasonally and stored until it is required. The new product should be one that can be produced with present plant facilities and machines and with the present working force. The advantages of dovetailing are obviously eliminated if the new product is so different that it requires different plant equipment, different skills on the part of workers, and different channels of distribution. In spite of these limitations many companies have found dovetailing quite profitable from the standpoint of employment stabilization and also from the standpoint of the value of the secondary product.

There are many interesting and stimulating examples of companies which have diversified and dovetailed their products as a means of expanding and stabilizing employment. St. James Manufacturing Company added a complete line of farm hardware to its regular line of incubators and brooders. As a result of this development and other programs, the company's unemployment compensation tax rate was reduced from 2.7 per cent to 1 per cent of payroll.

The Westinghouse Electric Corporation purchased a plastics plant to produce electrical parts and found that the output of the plant exceeded its needs. Faced with the alternative of reducing the capacity of the plant or developing new plastic products, the company went into the production of Mickey Mouse dishes, spoons, and tumblers. Many changes were required, including the development of a new sales organization. Some rubber companies have added shoes and coats to fill in the slack season for tires.

Until 1938 the Vick Chemical Company produced only Vaporub, nose drops, cough drops, and inhalers whose sales were highly seasonal. The company has recently carried out a diversification program which involved the purchase of William S. Merrell Company, a pharmaceutical manufacturer, Prince Matchabelli, Inc., a perfume house, and the Seaforth line of men's toiletries. This action has markedly reduced seasonal fluctuations in employment.

The greeting card business, which was originally quite seasonal, has been stabilized considerably by the development and promotion of birthday cards, anniversary greetings, and convalescent cards.

Some excellent examples of dovetailing may be found in the food industry, where consumer demand is quite stable but where many problems are presented by the fact that the raw materials are available only during certain seasons. Oscar Mayer and Company and Geo. A. Hormel & Company have stabilized employment by developing canned and cured meat products which reach their peak in sales during the summer when the production of fresh meats is at its lowest point. Hormel has also made progress by equipping departments to undertake unrelated production functions. Two departments with complementary fluctuations in work loads were combined, and each was equipped to do the work of the other department as well as its own work. The Campbell Soup Company has done an outstanding job of dovetailing its many seasonal products.

The Michigan Alkali Company has been able to offer steady employment to its men by coordinating and dovetailing three seasonal operations: (1) operation of one of its plants which is seasonal, (2) periodic overhauling of its rolling stock, (3) reconditioning of the company's boats during three months of the winter.

Development of New and Improved Products

The development of new products may both combat seasonality and expand the level of the company's sales and employment. In some

cases it may be necessary to eliminate products which are highly seasonal and substitute more stable products. Whenever it is possible
to make a choice, it is naturally desirable to develop items that may
be manufactured for stock rather than ones that must be manufactured to the specifications of each customer.

The development of new products is often effective in reducing
the effects of a depression on the company's sales and employment
level. While the demand for a specific commodity may reach saturation at times, the demand for goods in general never seems to be
satisfied.

Some products are affected less by depression than others. One of
the best protections that a company can have against depression is
to expand its sales and production into these relatively depression-
proof fields. In general, luxury goods are more affected by a depression than are the necessities. A company manufacturing fishing
tackle, for example, would be on safer ground if it could develop a
supplementary line of household utensils. Less expensive lines of
goods have greater stability both from the seasonal standpoint and
from the standpoint of the business cycle. Oneida, Ltd. sells its most
expensive grades of silverware during the Christmas season but has
developed a lower priced grade of silverware which can be used as
premiums and for sale to hotels and restaurants.

There are dangers, however, in introducing a new product during
a depression when competition for the buyer's dollar is very keen.
Diversification should be undertaken during periods of normal
business.

Research on Products and Processes

A research program will make a contribution to employment
stabilization. The new products discussed in the preceding section
can be developed and produced only by means of adequate research
programs. One company in the chemical industry reports that 50
per cent of its sales at the present time are in products less than ten
years old. Such figures indicate that research on new products and
processes is essential if a company is to progress or even hold its own.

Seasonal and cyclical fluctuations in sales and employment may
often be overcome by finding new uses for the company's products.
Through research on manufacturing processes a company must improve its product if it wishes to stay abreast of competition. Many
products have characteristics that limit their general acceptability
and usefulness. By reducing the number of these unfavorable charac-

teristics, of which high price may be one, the research program makes its contribution to the stability of the company.

The amount of a product that can be sold is closely related to the price of the product. If it is possible to develop through research more economical ways of making the product, these economies should be reflected in a lower price to the consumer. This reduced price will, in turn, result in higher levels of production and employment.

Practically all large manufacturing companies maintain a research staff. Small companies, on the other hand, often feel that they cannot afford a research organization. In view of the great contribution that research can make to operating efficiently and to maintaining a high stable level of employment, every manufacturer should have at least one person who gives attention to the improvement of products and processes. If this man is properly trained and if the company provides the necessary facilities and opportunities for research, the results are almost certain to be so profitable that the company will soon wish to expand the research program.

Many companies support an active research program when business is good and money is plentiful. When a depression comes, however, research activities are reduced or eliminated. Instead of reducing research activities during a depression it would be advisable to increase them. When sales are declining, there is a great need for new products, cheaper products, and new uses for old products. It would be wise, therefore, to set aside during periods of good business reserves earmarked for research purposes during periods of depression. Only in that way will it be possible for a company to maintain or expand research activities during the time when they are most needed.

The management of the company and the research staff must recognize employment stabilization as one of the desirable outcomes of a research program. If the research organization recognizes employment stabilization as one of its challenging problems, results may be achieved in terms of new products to fill in seasonal slumps, changes in products which will permit year-round sale, more economical and attractive packaging, new uses, and reduced costs. These results may seem to be no different from those which any company hopes to achieve through its research activities. Experience has shown, however, that when special attention is given employment stabilization problems by a research staff, more progress is made in this direction. After the passage of the Unemployment Compensation Law in Wisconsin, companies gave special attention to reducing fluctuations in employment. In many companies amazing progress was made in achieving a higher degree of employment stabilization because research workers and other production and staff departments were thinking and working along the lines of employment stabilization.

THE SALES PROGRAM

On the whole, steady production and steady jobs require correspondingly smooth distribution of the product. Production for stock is, at best, only a temporary solution to the problem of employment fluctuations. For this reason, companies striving for stable employment must give considerable attention to their sales policies, sales outlets, selection and training of salesmen, sales forecasts, market research, and advertising programs. Improvement in the sales program will be effective in reducing seasonal and cyclical fluctuations in employment.

Sales Policies

There are many ways in which sales policies can either decrease or exaggerate fluctuations in employment. For this reason, an employment stabilization program can be effective only if it has the full support of the top management of a company that is in a position to secure full cooperation from both the production department and the sales department. Some specific sales policies which will lead to regular production and stable employment are listed below:

1. Encourage customers to order regularly. By offering discounts on large orders, a company may be able to persuade customers to combine their orders into one large order with delivery spaced over a period of time. Salesmen may be able to convince customers that, in the long run, they pay for the irregularity of their orders.

2. Concentrate on standard items. Since it is much easier for a company to maintain stable employment if it manufactures a considerable proportion of stock goods, salesmen can help by pushing these stock items wherever possible. Production and employment are often lost because of orders that require special designs, set-ups, or equipment.

3. Expand the selling season. Many companies have decreased seasonal fluctuation in sales and employment by getting customers to buy in off seasons. The Hills Brothers Company, producer of dates, has produced a year-round demand for dates by educating customers regarding their many uses. Fuel dealers offer discounts to customers who buy their fuel in the spring. Organizations such as the Book-of-

the-Month Club increase the number of books sold by regularizing the purchase of books.

4. Schedule deliveries. By working closely with the manufacturing department, salesmen may be able to arrange satisfactory delivery dates for goods sold. If the goods are delivered as needed rather than in one delivery, employment can be stabilized somewhat for both the manufacturer and the customer. If the manufacturer is short of warehouse space for goods produced in slack seasons, arrangements can often be made whereby the customer will accept goods in advance of his actual need for them and will pay the manufacturer several weeks or even months later, at the time when he normally would have received the goods.

Distribution Outlets

The proper selection and development of channels for distributing the product will make a contribution to stabilizing a manufacturer's employment. It is known that some industries are less subject to fluctuations than others. Food, soap, petroleum, tobacco, and pharmaceutical products are especially stable. Manufacturers would do well to sell as high a percentage of their products as possible to companies in these stable fields. It is also known that some companies, through their purchasing policies, give greater protection and support to their suppliers than others do. A company's sales are best protected by diversifying the outlets. A manufacturer who sells his entire product to one manufacturer's agent or jobber is especially vulnerable to cutbacks.

In the early twenties the management of the Procter and Gamble Company found that, although consumption of soap remained essentially constant throughout the year, the buying habits of wholesalers caused wide fluctuation in the production of soap. The wholesalers bought heavily during the summer and winter months and curtailed their orders in spring and fall. The wholesalers also "played the market"—placed large orders when prices were rising and stopped buying when prices were dropping. In order to stabilize their sales and production, the Procter and Gamble Company began selling its product directly to retailers as well as to wholesalers. This change in policy necessitated the development of a large sales force.

Often a manufacturer can both increase and stabilize his sales by working closely with his wholesale and retail outlets. A manufacturer can often help his distributors improve their methods of selling, delivery, and inventory control. Another possibility is to carry the retailer's inventory at the factory for immediate shipment when needed rather than having the retailer stock up annually or semi-annually. In return for regularity of orders, some manufacturers have given certain retailers exclusive distribution of their products, improved inspection, and improved or special packaging. In order to stabilize employment, some manufacturers have found it desirable to control distribution through their own retail outlets. The Nunn-Bush Shoe Company is an example.

In attempting to expand and stabilize sales, a company should not overlook the opportunities offered by the foreign market. Manufacturers who export goods to South America, for example, often find that the peak seasons on exports dovetail nicely with the peak seasons in domestic sales. Manufacture for export may be inadvisable in some cases, however, because of many unusual problems presented by the export business, such as differences in style and sizes.

Selection, Training, and Compensation of Salesmen

Since the welfare of a business, including the stability of its employment, depends to such a large extent upon the effectiveness of the sales organization, much effort can profitably be spent on the selection of salesmen. In many companies, applicants for sales jobs are judged on the basis of an application blank and one interview with the sales manager. Companies wishing to improve the selection of salesmen will investigate more thoroughly the qualifications of each applicant by means of further interviews, aptitude tests, and checking on previous experience.

The goal of sales training is to give the company's salesmen the information, sales techniques, and enthusiasm needed to produce the largest volume of sales in the long run. To produce these results, a sales training program must be a continuous process. The training program must make full use of all the techniques available: conferences, demonstrations, in-field training, and various types of material regarding the company's sales program and products. The important role which salesmen play in providing stable employment for the workers of the company should be explained. If they understand the importance of reducing fluctuations in employment, salesmen will make greater efforts to arrange delivery dates that will not disrupt the production schedule and will make a special effort to sell goods that can be produced during slack seasons.

The company's compensation plan for salesmen has a great effect on their attitude and productiveness. A satisfactory compensation plan is needed to attract the highest type of salesmen and to motivate them to their best efforts. To encourage salesmen to give whole-hearted support to the employment stabilization program outlined here, proper recognition of these points should be given in the sales-man compensation plan. In the interest of full employment, this plan should be one that will encourage the highest volume of busi-ness on a year-round basis rather than one that encourages maxi-mum orders at one time. A compensation plan that encourages "high pressure" methods often causes wide fluctuation in sales, production, and employment. Also, in the interest of creating and sustaining a high level of employment, the compensation plan should encourage salesmen to develop new business and new terri-tory rather than simply to solicit business from established cus-tomers.

Advertising

Advertising can be a powerful influence in reducing seasonal fluc-tuations in employment and in maintaining sales and employment levels during a depression. A company should intensify its advertis-ing efforts when sales start to decline. In order to maintain a financial position which permits increased expenditures for advertising during periods of declining business, the company should set aside during periods of good business reserves which may be spent for advertising when needed.

There are some who decry expenditures for advertising on the grounds that it is an unproductive use of money. Advertising programs can be socially beneficial, however, if they result in increased sales, with accompanying increases in production and employment, and in decreased cost of the product to the consumer. The goal of both adver-tising and selling efforts should be to raise the consumption level and not simply to take customers away from competitors. The company's product and market will determine the distribution of the advertising budget among the various advertising media—radio, newspaper, mag-azine, and direct mail advertising.

An advertising program may help to reduce seasonal fluctuations in employment by changing the buying habits of customers, by increas-ing the off-season demand for products, by introducing fill-in prod-ucts, and by publicizing new uses for products. The fundamental contribution of advertising to full employment, however, is to in-crease the volume of business and the number of jobs available.

Examples of companies which have used advertising to expand and stabilize sales are numerous. The Radio Corporation of America, the Bausch and Lomb Optical Company, the Westinghouse Electric Corporation, and the Procter and Gamble Company are examples of companies that launch advertising campaigns to stimulate sales during dull seasons. Also, the manufacturers of Coca Cola, Canada Dry Ginger Ale, candy, cold cereals, and tires have created greater off-season demand for their products through advertising. Mail-order houses issue special catalogs to stimulate business during seasons which would otherwise be slack.

Price Policy

The decision must occasionally be made whether to price goods for maximum unit profit with a limited volume of sales or to accept a smaller unit profit on a larger volume of business. The larger volume of business is more desirable economically and socially because it will raise levels of consumption and employment.

Inducements of various kinds may be offered to encourage off-season buying of goods. Price reductions may help to keep production and employment at high levels if the demand for the goods is sufficiently responsive to price changes. To be effective the price reduction must be known to all prospective buyers. There are some disadvantages to off-season price reductions. For example, there is the possibility of offending buyers who already have purchased stocks or who, for some other reason, cannot take advantage of the price reduction. If these price reductions are made at the beginning of a cyclical depression, they may simply serve to accentuate the decline in business and prices. The price reduction may cause some buyers to expect further price reductions and for that reason it may delay their orders and operate in a direction opposite to that desired. In addition to price reductions, the most common inducements for off-season buying are deferred payment, premiums, and the privilege of returning unsold stock.

Market Research

Market research and analysis are tools that progressive managements can frequently use to improve sales and consequently to provide jobs for more people. Large manufacturers have their own market research departments, but small manufacturers must rely upon the services of market research consultants.

Through a study of its markets, a company may seek the answers to such questions as the following:

1. What changes have occurred recently in the market possibilities for the products?

2. What changes can be made in the product to satisfy better the needs of customers? Is the company taking full advantage of all the new materials and processes that have been developed recently?

3. How will recent population shifts affect the location of markets?

4. Is there an export market for the product?

5. Can distribution methods be simplified and made more profitable?

6. Should additional sales territories be developed?

Studies of the opinions of consumers may give the manufacturer valuable information regarding his product: new uses, modifications which will increase consumer appeal, and misconceptions which can be corrected through advertising. Thus, market research makes a real contribution to high levels of sales and employment by suggesting changes which will make the product acceptable to larger numbers of customers.

Market research may help also to reduce seasonal fluctuations in sales and employment. One aim of the research should be to find out why customers buy the products irregularly. There may be certain changes that can be made in the product to eliminate this seasonal buying. Perhaps some changes are needed in sales and advertising methods. Market research may also uncover possibilities for dovetailing of products.

Sales Forecasts

The cornerstone of all planned production and stabilized employment is an accurate forecast of sales. A company can produce goods for stock only if it knows with some accuracy the amount of each type of product which it can expect to sell during the next few months. These forecasts are based on sales for previous years after adjustments have been made for observable trend in sales of different products. Most companies review these sales forecasts monthly or quarterly, and necessary adjustments are made in production quotas and manpower. By careful study a manufacturer can determine certain bases for prediction which will be reasonably accurate. A greeting card manufacturer, for example, has found that the orders received during the first three weeks after salesmen start contacting customers is a good indication of the season's sales. This company has been able to regularize employment by producing for stock according to these sales predictions.

PERSONNEL PROCEDURES TO STABILIZE EMPLOYMENT

Some of the most common and most effective methods of stabilizing employment are techniques of managing the working force. Short-range fluctuations, in particular, may be reduced by coordination of the plant's hiring, layoff, transfer, and training of employees. Systematic planning and control of production depend on cooperation among management, supervision, and workers and therefore call for good personnel relationships throughout the organization. Only when all phases of the employee-employer relationship are harmonious will there be maximum productivity. Slowdowns, strikes, and other demonstrations of employee dissatisfaction not only cause temporary interruptions in production and employment but also may increase costs to the point where the competitive position of the company will be weakened. A company whose efficiencies are low and whose costs are high will be among the first to lose business and reduce employment during a depression.

Centralized Control of Employment

In some companies a lack of coordination leads to the layoff of workers in one department at the same time that workers are being employed in another department. Most companies have centralized the responsibility for employment in one department. Department heads inform the employment department of their plans to release workers or to add additional workers to the force. When this is done, the employment department can attempt to fill vacancies with workers who would otherwise be laid off. Charles A. Myers' study of employment stabilization in Wisconsin[4] indicated that centralizing employment and layoff in one department helps to stabilize employment.

Perhaps the main reason for centralizing employment in one department is that the employment department can make better use of the various techniques in employment work than each department head could in his own department. The employment department can develop procedures, staff, and facilities for recruiting a higher grade of applicants and for determining the suitability of each applicant for employment by means of interviews, aptitude tests, and evaluation of previous experience. In the interest of employment stabilization, peo-

[4]Charles A. Myers, *Economic Stabilization and the Wisconsin Act* (Washington: U. S. Social Security Board, Employment Security Bureau, Research and Stabilization Division, 1940).

ple hired for one job should be capable of doing other jobs or should be capable of being trained for them. Employees are too often laid off when there are other jobs available in the factory simply because they do not have the necessary ability to fill these jobs. Some of this loss could be prevented by an appraisal of the abilities and potentialities of each applicant before he is hired.

An employment department can make a contribution by setting up employment standards and seeing that each vacancy is filled by the most capable person available at the time. The hiring of workers can be coordinated better with the long-range needs of the company when employment is centralized in one department. It is easier for a sales forecast to be translated into planned increases or reductions in the work force if one department has responsibility for employment.

Assigning to the employment department the responsibility for hiring, transfer, and layoff does not necessarily deprive the department head of the right to decide whether a particular employee will work in his department. Similarly, a department head must have the right to request that an unsatisfactory employee be removed from his department. The employment department must then decide whether it is desirable to place the employee in another department.

Training

A good training program results in increased efficiency of production and in a lower labor turnover rate. If there is a satisfactory training program in operation for each job, many vacancies can be filled by transfers which would otherwise have to be filled by hiring new people from outside the company. Employees often quit because they are discouraged with the progress they are making or with the rate of pay their level of skill permits them to earn. Employees are often discharged because they are not making satisfactory progress or are laid off because they do not know how to perform the jobs that are available. Since trained workers are more productive, a training program may result in lower unit costs, which will enable the company to maintain relatively high levels of sales and employment during a depression. All of these facts combine to indicate that training is an important employment stabilization technique.

There are four types of training, each of which has a contribution to make to employment stabilization: orientation, job training, apprenticeship training, and supervisory training. Like many other stabilization techniques, training is a management responsibility that falls ultimately on the individual department head.

Forty per cent of the companies covered in the Conference Board study indicated that they used training as a stabilization technique. There are numerous examples of companies in which training and transfer are the principal employment stabilization techniques. A company manufacturing rubber and canvas footwear reduced its annual labor turnover from 65 per cent to 10-15 per cent over a period of years by training employees so they could serve alternately as canvas stitchers and rubber footwear operators. McCormick and Company, Inc. maintains a training program to support its policy of transfer. Production workers are trained to do building and maintenance and repair work during slack production periods. The Dennison Manufacturing Company (paper products) reports that it spends more time in training for transfer than in training new employees.

Transfer of Employees

The companies covered in the Conference Board study indicated that they used transfer of workers more often than any other stabilization method except production of goods for stock. Although transfer of workers is widely used as an employment stabilization technique, such a program will be successful only if certain requirements are met. Workers must be versatile in the sense that they either have skills to perform several different jobs or have the ability to learn those skills easily. Workers, furthermore, must be willing to accept transfer and must cooperate in learning the new work. This attitude on the part of workers can be achieved best if a full explanation is given to them of the objectives and procedures of employment stabilization in the company. Another requirement for a successful transfer program is a thorough study of the jobs in the factory to indicate which ones are similar enough to make transfer of workers feasible. Transfer of workers will be facilitated if a list is prepared showing groups of similar jobs. Extensive use of transfer is possible only if there is a satisfactory training program for each job. Seniority provisions in union contracts must be flexible enough to permit transfer from one job to another and from one department to another. Seniority, in other words, must be accumulated on a plant-wide basis. Plant-wide seniority is a concession that unions must make in return for the company's effort to stabilize employment. A policy regarding paying transferred workers must be carefully worked out. The most common policy is to pay the transferee at the rate of pay prevailing on his new job. In case the new job pays a lower rate, however, the employee may be paid the rate of pay which he had been receiving on his old job. Especially would this be true if the transfer was arranged for a short period of time or for the convenience of management. In any case the rate of pay for transferees must be one that can be justified to the employee and to his fellow workers if necessary.

In spite of the difficulties to be overcome in working out a program of transfer, the efforts of many companies have been successful. Transfer has played a large part in the successful stabilization program of such companies as the Procter and Gamble Company, Spiegel, Inc., and McCormick and Company, Inc. McCormick and Company has an outstanding transfer program; it makes a great effort to hire capable, versatile people and then trains them so that they may be transferred to meet the peak demands of various departments. A man may be transferred from a production department to the office or even to a selling job.

The Atlantic Refining Company reduces labor turnover and provides a supply of skilled labor for the vacation period by transferring drivers of fuel oil trucks at the end of the winter heating season to jobs in the refinery where they take the places of employees on vacation. Thompson Products, Inc., estimates that 50 per cent of its workers have at some time worked on jobs other than their regular ones as the result of the company's policy of never laying off an employee if he can be transferred.

It would be a mistake, however, to believe that a transfer program will always be successful. Geo. A. Hormel & Company, for example, tried to develop extra skills among employees so that an entire gang could work part of the day on one job and the rest of the day on another job. The company found that this plan did not work satisfactorily because the men objected to being transferred from one job to another in this way.

Employer-Employee Relations

Good relationships between an employer and his employees are an asset to the company in striving to maintain its competitive position. Satisfied workers who trust the motives of management and who are convinced that the progress of the company will benefit them will be more productive and cooperative in every way. One of the most critical interruptions to production and employment is a work stoppage resulting from a labor-management dispute. No attempt will be made here to outline a program for harmonious relationships between management and labor, but the problem should be recognized as one which is related to the problem of employment stabilization. Good labor relations are built on sound personnel policies and practices, consistent and impartial administration of policies, and open channels of communication between management and workers.

One of the recurrent problems of employer-employee relations is the reluctance of employees to accept technological change. Workers may be able to understand the general fact that a continually increasing standard of living for the nation as a whole requires continual improvement of methods and continual reduction of costs. This general fact, however, is not very consoling to the individual worker who sees his own job security threatened by the introduction of new methods or machines. To meet competition on price and quality, a manufacturer must introduce technological improvements as they occur. Furthermore, he must introduce these changes in such a way as to encounter minimum resistance from his employees. Effective methods for dealing with this problem include explanation of the need for the change, training programs to fit workers for new jobs, and other efforts to avoid layoff of workers.

The Flexible Work Week

Reducing the number of hours in the work week is the most common method of adjusting to reduced production demands without laying off workers. If an employer has more workers than he can keep employed, he can do nothing but dismiss some of the workers or reduce the length of the work week. Strictly speaking, spreading the available work among all the employees on the payroll cannot be considered a stabilization technique since the total amount of employment is decreased. From the standpoint of providing some income for all employees, however, it is probably desirable to reduce the work week to a certain point.

During the recession of 1938 a number of employers in Cincinnati reduced hours rather than the number of employees. When demand for products increased in a few months, these employers did not have to hire and train new workers but simply lengthened the number of hours worked each week.

McCormick and Company, Inc., of Baltimore uses a flexible work week to fulfill its guarantee of forty-eight weeks of work, including vacation, for all employees with six or more months of service. The hours of work per week are not guaranteed, however, and when necessary the hours per week are reduced rather than the number of employees or the number of work weeks per year.

A problem in employment stabilization arises when a manufacturer receives an order so large that he cannot produce it with his present employees working forty hours a week. The employer may hire temporary workers, have present employees work longer hours, or refuse the order. A company which wished to achieve the maximum stabilization of employment would increase the number of workers only when the expansion was in line with the long-range trend of the business. This is an extreme position, and one which few companies take.

Just as the work week may be shortened during temporary slumps in business, it may also be lengthened during temporary booms. This flexibility in the length of the work week stabilizes employment by making it unnecessary to lay off regular employees during slumps in business or to hire temporary workers during periods of high activity. For many years there have been no layoffs in one machine manufacturing company owing primarily to a conservative sales policy and to the practice of allowing the permanent staff to work overtime during peak periods rather than temporarily increasing the number of workers.

Vacation Policy

Practically all industrial and business establishments now have annual vacations with pay for employees. Vacations may be used as an employment stabilization procedure since they introduce an element of flexibility into the employment plans of a company. In times of high production demands and manpower shortages, employees may be asked to accept cash in place of actually taking time off for vacation. Experience during the war showed that under such conditions practically all employees take the money rather than the time. If, on the other hand, business is not good, management and labor may agree that all employees shall be asked to take time off from work during the vacation period. Some companies shut the plant down during the vacation period each year so that substitutes will not have to be hired to work during this time. Employment stability is achieved at the cost of reducing the total amount of production and employment.

Emergency Labor Groups

It is a common practice to meet the fluctuating demands for manpower by forming a special group made up of workers who can do several different jobs when the need arises. People from this group are assigned to work in the place of employees on vacation or absent for other reasons, and to meet special production requirements and other emergencies. Such a labor pool serves to stabilize employment, since it makes it unnecessary for the company to hire people for temporary work who will have to be laid off in a few days. Another valuable result is that the personnel department can devote more time and attention to filling vacancies and arranging transfers. When not engaged in emergency work, these men may do maintenance work or some other type of deferred work. A paper-making company in Wisconsin reduced its unemployment compensation tax rate from 2.7 per cent to 1 per cent, saving the company $1,700 per month, by the use of two procedures: transfer of workers back and forth between production and maintenance departments and improved cooperation from customers and salesmen in timing orders.

Geo. A. Hormel & Company places new employees in an extra gang. These employees are tagged for certain departments and become substitutes for absentees and workers on vacation. During peak seasons, members in this extra gang are assigned to departments in which they have already had experience.

A UNIFIED PROGRAM

This chapter has described the various methods that a company may use in expanding and stabilizing employment. No one company will find it necessary or feasible to use all of these procedures. An analysis of the company's sales, production, and employment figures will indicate the sources of fluctuations and the measures most likely to be effective in reducing these fluctuations.

The next chapter contains case studies of companies that have been successful in stabilizing employment by utilizing methods appropriate to their situation.

REFERENCES

American Legion. Employment Stabilization Service. *To Make Jobs More Steady and to Make More Steady Jobs.* St. Paul, Minn.: Webb Publishing Co., 1942. Various pagination.

Association of Consulting Management Engineers. *Planning the Future of Your Business.* Handbook for Industry No. 1. New York: Committee for Economic Development, 1944. Pp. 23.

Brower, F. Beatrice. *Annual Wage and Employment Guarantee Plans.* Studies in Personnel Policy No. 76. New York: National Industrial Conference Board, 1946. Pp. 55.

———. *Reducing Fluctuations in Employment; Experience in 31 Industries.* Studies in Personnel Policy No. 27. New York: National Industrial Conference Board, 1940. Pp. 60.

Committee for Economic Development. International Trade Committee. *Handbook on International Trade for Manufacturers, Wholesalers, Jobbers, Retailers.* New York: The Committee, 1946. Pp. 100.

Deupree, Richard R. "Management's Responsibility toward Stabilized Employment," in *Management Planning for Employment Stabilization.* General Management Series No. 135. New York: American Management Association, 1945. Pp. 3-9.

Myers, Charles A. *Economic Stabilization and the Wisconsin Act.* Employment Security Memorandum No. 10. Washington: U. S. Social Security Board, Employment Security Bureau, Research and Stabilization Division, 1940. Pp. 149. Processed.

Thompson, Laura A. *The Guaranteed Annual Wage and Other Proposals for Steadying the Worker's Income: Selected References.* Washington: U. S. Department of Labor Library, 1945. Pp. 19. Processed.

4

Employment Stabilization in
the Individual Company

IN THE PREVIOUS CHAPTER, the various stabilization methods were considered separately without regard to how they fit together into a stabilization program for a particular company. It is desirable to consider now what experience companies have had in adapting and combining stabilization methods to meet their particular stabilization problems. It is clear that each company must build for itself a stabilization program based on a study of employment conditions and trends, products, competitive conditions, and other characteristics of the company. To illustrate how companies have developed stabilization programs this chapter will describe the experiences of ten companies, each in a different industry.

STUDIES OF EMPLOYMENT STABILIZATION

The outstanding studies of employment stabilization methods have been made by the National Industrial Conference Board, the American Management Association, and the American Legion Employment Stabilization Service. The complete references to their published reports are given at the end of this chapter. The examples cited here are taken largely from these sources. It is unfortunate that these examples deal exclusively with the efforts of companies to combat short-range fluctuations in employment. There are few, if any, published reports of the experience of companies in combating cyclical fluctuations in employment.

In 1940, as discussed above, the National Industrial Conference Board obtained information from 203 companies regarding their experiences with stabilization procedures.[1] The methods most frequently used for stabilizing employment were manufacture for stock, transfer and training of workers, and the use of the flexible work

[1]F. Beatrice Brower, *op. cit.*

week. Other common measures were introduction of new products or new models, special advertising campaigns, and inducements to place orders in off seasons.

Between 1940 and 1942 the American Legion Employment Stabilization Service made a study of 109 companies with stabilization programs.[2] From 79 employers they were able to secure data regarding employment in the company before and after adopting employment stabilization procedures. Before employment stabilization these 79 employers provided only 44 per cent as many man-hours of work in the lowest week of the year as they did in the week of highest production. The corresponding figure after employment stabilization was 68 per cent. From the standpoint of the number of people employed, a similar improvement was made. The number of people employed during the average month increased from 80 per cent of peak employment to 93 per cent. The principal stabilization methods used by the companies cooperating in the American Legion study were: centralized personnel control, deferred maintenance, production for stock, transfer of workers, diversification of products, and off-season selling.

TABLE I

EXPERIENCE OF COMPANIES BEFORE AND AFTER EMPLOYMENT STABILIZATION

Type of Business	Stability of Man-Hours* Before Per cent	Stability of Man-Hours* After Per cent	Unemployment Compensation Tax Rate Before Per cent	Unemployment Compensation Tax Rate After Per cent
Meat Packing	63	70	3.2	0.5
Toy Manufacturing	29	37	4.0	2.0
Shoe Manufacturing	80	80	4.0	1.0
Textile Manufacturing	74	85	2.7	1.0
Candy Manufacturing	37	55	2.7	1.0
Garment Manufacturing	6	19	4.0	1.0
Sausage Manufacturing	58	72	2.7	1.0
Leather Tanning	61	100	2.7	1.0
Machinery Manufacturing	59	77	2.7	1.0

*Man-hours worked in lowest week divided by man-hours worked in peak week.

Table I shows some of the results achieved by employment stabilization programs in 9 companies included in the American Legion study. The American Legion study indicated further that, in a group of 15 companies, stabilization of employment had resulted in an average saving in unemployment compensation tax equivalent to 2.25 per cent of payroll, 0.82 per cent of gross sales, and 2.94 per cent of invested capital.

In 1945 the American Management Association published a study

[2]American Legion, Employment Stabilization Service, *To Make Jobs More Steady and to Make More Steady Jobs* (St. Paul, Minn.: Webb Publishing Co., 1942).

of annual wage plans and employment stabilization techniques.[3] The following conclusions were made regarding the use of employment stabilization techniques:

1. Each company should have information regarding fluctuations in its sales, production, and employment.

2. There should be a constant search for ways of making employment more regular.

3. The most effective methods for reaching a higher level of employment are cost reduction and research.

4. Almost every company can increase the stability of its employment by improving production, personnel, and marketing policies and practices.

5. The particular characteristics and problems of the company will determine whether additional benefits can be achieved through customer education, production for stock, and the development of new products for dovetailing purposes.

6. Expenditures for additional plant and equipment should be spaced so as to regularize employment for the particular company and for the company's suppliers.

7. Industry can make more progress toward regularizing employment under favorable government policies and practices in the fields of taxation, banking, foreign trade, etc.

8. Finally, much depends upon the development and continuation of a hopeful, constructive, enterprising, and cooperative state of mind on the part of businessmen and other citizens.

Another study that should be mentioned is that which Charles A. Myers of the Massachusetts Institute of Technology conducted during 1937-38 in Wisconsin (*op. cit.*). He found that employers in that state had been motivated by the Wisconsin Unemployment Compensation Act to stabilize employment in the following ways:

1. Hiring fewer people during peak seasons.

2. Manufacture for stock.

3. Deferred maintenance and repair work.

4. Transfers and retraining.

5. Centralized employment practices.

CASE STUDIES

In the next few pages consideration will be given to the programs of some companies which have been successful in stabilizing employ-

---

[3]Ernest Dale, *Annual Wages and Employment Stabilization Techniques* (New York: American Management Association, 1945).

ment. No two programs are the same because the conditions and problems of companies are different.

The Procter and Gamble Company

The Procter and Gamble Company has been unusually successful in stabilizing employment. The underlying principle behind the plan has been the idea that goods which are consumed evenly should be produced evenly rather than unevenly to follow fluctuations in buying of the product. In order to carry out this policy, the company had to change its sales program so that goods were sold to retailers as well as wholesalers. Furthermore, only noncancellable orders are accepted for delivery. Under this arrangement, orders do not have to be shipped as soon as they are received, but deliveries may be spaced over a period of months. It has been necessary to erect or rent warehouses to take care of goods produced during periods when retailers and wholesalers permit their orders to lag behind consumption.

In 1923, after reorganizing sales policies and methods, the Procter and Gamble Company guaranteed all employees with two years of service not less than forty-eight weeks of work in each calendar year. This guarantee has been fulfilled each year, and the cost of maintaining the program has been no more than 3 per cent of annual payroll in the most difficult year. Richard R. Deupree, president of the Procter and Gamble Company, reports the results of their plan to be as follows:[4] (1) more units are produced per man-hour; (2) employees are more receptive to new production methods; (3) a saving is realized by purchasing material steadily; (4) a saving of $100,000,000 in plant investment resulted from the fact that a steady operation can produce the same amount of goods with a smaller plant; and (5) there is a definite improvement in employee relations.

Standard Oil Company (New Jersey)

The Standard Oil Company (New Jersey) has also been successful in providing steady employment. The extent of the efforts to stabilize employment is illustrated by the manner in which the company attacked seasonal fluctuations. A study in 1926 showed that there was a decided slump in the sale of gasoline and motor oil from December to March of each year. In order to provide some steady winter business, the company tackled the problem of developing oil as a fuel for heating homes. Before oil could be used as a home fuel it was necessary to develop a serviceable automatic oil burner for homes. When this was

---

[4]Richard R. Deupree, *op. cit.*, pp. 6-8.

accomplished, the home fuel oil business reduced the peaks and valleys in the sales and production of the Standard Oil Company. Refinery workers and tanker crews are now kept busy year-round, meeting the peak demands for motor oil and gasoline during nine months of the year and the demand for fuel oil during the remaining months of the year. The development of storage facilities makes it possible to store gasoline in the winter months and heating oil in the summer months.

Oneida, Ltd.

Oneida, Ltd., producer of silverware, has made considerable progress toward stabilizing employment in the following ways:
1. Forecasting sales.
2. Manufacturing for stock.
3. Postdating terms on early shipments.
4. Adopting a flexible work week.
5. Producing a lower priced grade of silverware which can be used as premiums.
6. Securing year-round business from hotels and restaurants.

Wisconsin Foundry

A foundry in Wisconsin cut its layoff rate in half by carrying out three policies. First, price concessions were given for large orders with deliveries spaced over a period of time. Then, workers were trained so that they could be transferred to different jobs when necessary. Finally, when production was decreased, the work week was reduced to as low as twenty-four hours before employees were laid off.

Machinery Manufacturer

A company making a wide variety of machinery for home, farm, and industrial use reduced labor turnover from 31.9 per cent in 1930 to 9.5 per cent in 1939 by utilizing the following stabilization methods:
1. Training to permit transfer.
2. Flexible work week.
3. Manufacture for stock.
4. Postponement of maintenance work.

Building Material Manufacturer[5]

Because of the great fluctuation in the building industry, employ-

[5]American Legion, Employment Stabilization Service, *op. cit.*, Case No. 28.

ment stabilization in this field is difficult. Nevertheless, this company, motivated by the experience-rating provision of the state unemployment compensation law, made progress in stabilizing employment. Study of the company's operation indicated that tax savings might be great enough to exceed the cost of production for stock including the construction of a new warehouse.

The principal stabilization method used is production for stock. This production is based upon careful estimates of sales which are revised periodically. To permit manufacture for stock during the midwinter and midsummer slack seasons, the company built a large warehouse.

Results of the stabilization program have been satisfactory. Continuous operation has permitted the company to increase its volume of production 20 per cent with no increase in investment except for the new warehouse which increased plant investment by 4.2 per cent. The saving in overhead cost per unit of production is approximately 12 per cent. Management of the company believes that the employment stabilization program has resulted in great improvement in the company's safety experience. During the period when employment stabilization was being achieved (1935-40), the accident rate in the plant decreased each year and the premium rate for workmen's compensation insurance dropped from $5.60 to $2.40 per $100 of payroll.

STABILIZATION DATA

	1934 Per cent	1939 Per cent
EMPLOYMENT*		
Man-hours		
Peak week	100	100
Average week	45	89
Low week	0	82
Persons		
Peak week	100	100
Average week	65	91
Low week	0	90
Continuously employed	0	90
VOLUME OF SALES		
Peak week	100	100
Average week	14	17
Low week	0	0
UNEMPLOYMENT COMPENSATION TAX RATE . . .	4†	1

*Factory workers only, exclusive of supervisory staff.
†This rate is estimated as the liability of the company if the unemployment compensation law had been in effect in 1934. Similar estimates are made whenever necessary for other companies discussed in this section.

This tax reduction amounted to a saving of 3.2 per cent of payroll. An additional 2.7 per cent of payroll was saved in 1940 as a result of reduced unemployment compensation tax. The amount of money saved on unemployment compensation tax alone in 1940 exceeded the cost of the new warehouse. Before the employment stabilization program was started, none of the company's plant employees had continuous employment throughout the year. After the stabilization program was in effect nine men out of ten had steady jobs throughout the year. Additional indications of the results of the stabilization program are given in the table on p. 53.

Automotive Parts Manufacturer[6]

Efforts to stabilize employment in this company were made difficult by the seasonal demand and by the fact that it was difficult to predict demand from year to year. By liberal credit terms on orders received ahead of the usual sales season, the company obtains a sound basis for predicting sales for the coming year. Based on this prediction production for stock is undertaken.

The customers were offered December shipments on orders placed in September and October, with payments due in three equal installments on January 1, February 1, and March 1. This offer was sufficiently liberal to bring in enough orders to form a basis for a prediction of the coming year's business. This method cost less, however,

STABILIZATION DATA

	1935 Per cent	1939 Per cent
EMPLOYMENT		
Man-hours		
Peak month	100	100
Average month	75	79
Low month	52	62
Persons		
Peak month	100	100
Average month	79	98
Low month	61	98
Continuously employed	61	98
VOLUME OF SALES		
Peak month	100	100
Average month	54	64
Low month	16	38
UNEMPLOYMENT COMPENSATION TAX RATE	2.7	1

[6]American Legion, Employment Stabilization Service, *op. cit.*, Case No. 46.

than it would have cost to offer an inducement liberal enough to bring in enough orders to fill the slack season.

Costs involved in carrying a larger inventory and in carrying larger accounts receivable represent only 0.69 per cent of annual sales. Savings from stabilization, on the other hand, include a 2 per cent reduction in manufacturing costs, an 8 per cent reduction in labor costs, and a saving of 1.7 per cent of payroll in unemployment compensation tax. The company estimates that the 1939 saving equaled a return of $9.15 per share of common stock with a book value of approximately $600. Additional results of the employment stabilization program are shown in the table on p. 54.

Furniture Manufacturer[7]

The new management of this company found that both employee morale and profits had suffered from the irregular employment resulting from the policy of manufacturing furniture only as orders were received. Slack periods when regular employees were laid off alternated with rush periods when extra help had to be hired. The cost of training new employees was approximately 4 per cent of gross annual sales.

STABILIZATION DATA

	1936 Per cent	1939 Per cent
EMPLOYMENT		
Man-hours		
Peak month	100	100
Average month	53	66
Low month	25	51
Persons		
Peak month	100	100
Average month	60	84
Low month	42	73
Continuously employed	68	97
VOLUME OF PRODUCTION		
Peak month	100	100
Average month	56	85
Low month	23	72
VOLUME OF SALES		
Peak month	100	100
Average month	56	67
Low month	23	48
UNEMPLOYMENT COMPENSATION TAX RATE . . .	2.7	1

[7]American Legion, Employment Stabilization Service, *op. cit.*, Case No. 48.

Employment stabilization has been achieved primarily by the use of three methods. Each worker is trained so that he can perform at least two different jobs. From the former policy of producing only what had been sold, the company has shifted to manufacturing for stock those items which are expected to be in greatest demand based upon past experience. A special discount is given to customers who purchase more than a certain amount during the six months when business is slack.

Management of this company has been well rewarded for its stabilization efforts. Reduced training costs have amounted to 3.5 per cent of gross annual sales. Workers' production per hour rose 50 per cent during the first four years of stabilization, while overhead costs per unit fell 19 per cent. Additional results of the stabilization program are shown in the table on p. 55.

Farm Equipment Manufacturer[8]

In order to reduce overhead expense per unit of product without regard for employment stabilization, the company added a new line of machinery which had a seasonal peak during the slow months for the original products. The incidental effect of this new product, of course, was to stabilize employment to some extent. After the passage of the state unemployment compensation law, the company made an effort to spread production and employment evenly over the twelve months

STABILIZATION DATA

	1929 Per cent	1939 Per cent
EMPLOYMENT		
Man-hours (estimates)		
Peak week	100	100
Average week	65	86
Low week	27	69
Persons		
Peak week	100	100
Average week	83	90
Low week	61	81
Continuously employed	61	89
VOLUME OF SALES		
Peak week	100	100
Average week	25	44
Low week	5	21
UNEMPLOYMENT COMPENSATION TAX RATE . . .	2.7*	1

*Estimated rate, had the law been in effect at that time.

[8]American Legion, Employment Stabilization Service, *op. cit.*, Case No. 63.

of the year. Production for stock was undertaken based on careful sales estimates. Workers are transferred from one job to another as the products change, but little training is required because most of the products are made on the same machines.

The addition of the new product and the spreading of production and employment evenly over twelve months have resulted in increased volume of business and a proportionate reduction in overhead costs per unit. In addition, the new product gave greater stability to the business. In fact, the new product is credited by the management with keeping the company in business during a nationwide drought which killed crops, reduced farm income, and reduced the demand for the company's other products. These benefits are in addition to the results shown in the table on p. 56.

Heating Equipment Manufacturer[9]

Employment stabilization was a real challenge for this company because normally more than 50 per cent of a year's shipments are made in the three fall months. Efforts were made to overcome the difficulties, however, in order to benefit plant employees. Reduced unemployment compensation taxes did not serve as an incentive in this case because the state law makes no provision for experience rating.

Results have been achieved through production for stock based on detailed sales forecasts. In manufacturing for stock, the company produces first standard parts which are interchangeable among several different models. To hold down investment in finished goods those products are produced first in which the labor cost is relatively high compared with the cost of materials.

Since this company's efforts to stabilize employment have extended over a thirty-year period, it is impossible to appraise the results accurately. The management of the company estimates, however, that the results have well repaid the efforts toward stabilization. It is estimated, for example, that if the company were operating on the old seasonal basis it would require a plant twice as large as the present one to do the same volume of business. The stabilization program has practically eliminated layoff and has so stabilized the work week at forty hours that practically no overtime payments are necessary. Further economies are realized from the longer machine runs which are possible when production is based on sales estimates. The cost of carrying a larger inventory is the only expense which the company pays for the benefits listed above and for those shown on p. 58.

[9]American Legion, Employment Stabilization Service, *op. cit.*, Case No. 92.

STABILIZATION DATA

EMPLOYMENT	1910 Per cent (estimated)	1940 Per cent
Man-hours		
Peak week	100	100
Average week	75	96
Low week	34	93
Persons		
Peak week	100	100
Average week	83	96
Low week	67	93
Continuously employed	67	99
VOLUME OF SHIPMENTS		
Peak month	100	100
Average month	46	46
Low month	19	19

PLANS FOR GUARANTEED EMPLOYMENT

As the culmination of their efforts to stabilize employment, some companies make a guarantee to employees regarding the amount of employment or wages that will be provided during a given period. Experience indicates, however, that such a guarantee is possible only after considerable progress has been made toward stabilizing employment. Recently there has been much interest in employment security plans, of which there are four types:

1. Employment guarantee plans. Part or all of the employees in a plant are guaranteed a certain number of weeks of work each year, based on a standard work week. Procter and Gamble Company and Spiegel, Inc. have such plans.

2. Annual wage plans. Under such plans employees get a certain amount of money each week regardless of the number of hours worked. Such plans usually guarantee further that employees will receive this pay for a fixed number of weeks each year. Nunn-Bush Shoe Company and Geo. A. Hormel & Company have such plans.

3. Wage-advance plan. Such plans operate by means of cash loans advanced against future earnings. General Motors Corporation had such a plan at one time.

4. Limited income-security plan. These plans are limited either in the proportion of employees covered, in the proportion of wages guaranteed, or in the period of time for which the guarantee extends. The Wm. Wrigley, Jr., Company, for example, guarantees a certain number of hours work each week while employed plus dismissal compensation if laid off.

Although employment stabilization can be recommended without qualification, each company must make a careful study of its own situation to determine whether it is possible and advisable to adopt an employment security plan. Some factors that must be considered in deciding whether it is possible to make a guarantee of employment or wages are listed below:

1. The certainty with which future sales can be predicted.

2. The competitive position of the company.

3. The extent to which stabilization of employment has already been achieved.

4. The extent to which labor may be expected to cooperate in making the employment guarantee work. Labor must make some concessions in terms of plant-wide seniority, greater productivity, fewer work stoppages, and possibly even reduced hourly rates.

A study by the National Industrial Conference Board covered the employment security plans of 61 companies.[10] Thirty-two of the 61 companies had discontinued their plans. Only 8 of the 29 active plans had been in effect more than ten years. The principal reasons given for the discontinuance of plans were union attitudes, wartime conditions, and the depression. In general, employment security plans are not appreciated during good times because no payments are made to employees under the plan. During a depression, on the other hand, employment security plans have a difficult time to survive. In the National Industrial Conference Board study, 9 plans were included that had been started before 1929. Seven of these 9 plans were discontinued during the depression because of the impossibility of meeting commitments under the plans.

The study of this same subject by the American Management Association[11] raised some question regarding the prospect for guaranteed employment and guaranteed wage plans, saying in part: "Guaranteed wages can be best applied where they are least needed; but where they are most needed they can be least applied." It should be emphasized that this pessimistic conclusion refers to guaranteed wage plans and not to employment stabilization itself. The American Management Association report concluded that practically all employers could benefit from an employment stabilization program even though the results of the stabilization program were not sufficient to warrant the adoption of an employment security guarantee.

---

[10]F. Beatrice Brower, *Annual Wage and Employment Guarantee Plans* (New York: National Industrial Conference Board, 1946).

[11]Ernest Dale, *op. cit.*

Before adopting an employment guarantee of any kind, a company will want to determine the liability which it is assuming under the plan. The effect of employment security plans on total costs will be less when labor costs are a small proportion of total costs, when machinery cannot easily be substituted for labor, when the demand for the product is not responsive to any great extent to price changes, and when the firm's sales are growing.

Some flexibility is possible in adapting the particular guarantee to the needs of an individual company because of the fact that guarantee plans can differ in at least the following three respects: the period of time the guarantee covers; the proportion of employees covered; and the amount of employment or wages guaranteed. It must be emphasized, however, that the guarantee will mean nothing to the employees unless it goes somewhat beyond the amount of employment which they could normally expect to have. It is this feature of guarantee plans which presents difficulties. There are some who feel that the guarantee will mean very little to employees unless the company goes beyond safe limits in making a guarantee.

Cooperation among Companies on Employment Stabilization

If companies striving to stabilize employment will cooperate, a higher degree of stabilization can be achieved. Through the cooperative efforts of employers, the employment level in a community can be both expanded and stabilized. In the case of a community more clearly than in the case of individual companies, it can be seen that stabilized employment will contribute to the development of high levels of employment. Workers with regular income provide an expanded market for goods and services. It is advantageous, therefore, for companies to help one another reduce fluctuations in employment.

There are many small companies in every community that cannot afford to maintain a staff to do research and to give expert services and advice in the fields of production, finance, sales, and personnel management. In many cases, it will be beneficial for all companies in a community to support jointly an organization to render such services. The Industrial Bureau of the Worcester, Massachusetts, Chamber of Commerce is an illustration of such an organization. The services rendered by this bureau are of the following types:

1. Production, accounting, and sales counsel.
2. Assistance in arranging financial credit.
3. Assistance in developing foreign trade.

4. Assistance with the patenting and production of local inventions.
5. Promoting the town as a site for industry and business.
6. Providing business information services.

Improvement in quality and reduction in price of a community's products will result in increased production and employment in the community. Furthermore, when the manufacturers in a community are in a good competitive position with respect to quality and price compared with other companies in their respective industries, the prospects for the community during a depression are improved.

Companies in a community can cooperate in other ways. It is often helpful to hold local conferences where companies that have had experience in stabilizing employment can present their methods and results. In some communities, cooperating companies borrow work or manpower from each other on a contract basis in order to provide work for their people or to avoid hiring extra people for special jobs. An excellent example of cooperative efforts to stabilize employment is the Employment Stabilization Bureau of Lorain County, Ohio. This organization was formed in 1938 by 15 employers in and near Elyria, Ohio. The membership of the organization has now increased to 28 plants. The Employment Stabilization Bureau refers unemployed workers of member plants to other plants in the group that have job vacancies. The organization also offers service to members in the fields of unemployment compensation and workmen's compensation. This program was based on a study of seasonal and cyclical fluctuations in the employment of each member company. Although there were seasonal fluctuations in the employment curve of some of the individual companies, the curve showing total employment of all member companies showed no seasonal fluctuation. The research showed also that seasonal layoff affected principally the unskilled and semiskilled workers who did not require extensive training and could, therefore, be transferred without much difficulty from one plant to another. As a part of this whole program, the individual companies made efforts to stabilize their own employment.

EXECUTION OF THE EMPLOYMENT STABILIZATION PROGRAM

The responsibility for achieving the highest possible degree of employment stabilization rests with the management of the individual company. Since this responsibility is just one of many responsibilities which management has, the execution of a stabilization program must be carried out by a staff man whose time may be devoted to this important area of management. Employment stabilization methods cut across all departments—production, distribution, research, and personnel—and there is, therefore, a need for one person to coordinate the efforts of the company in stabilizing employment.

One of the first duties of the "employment stabilization coordinator" will be to study all pertinent facts regarding the company's experience in production, sales, and employment. Special attention will be given to seasonal and cyclical fluctuations. Estimates should be made regarding the cost of these fluctuations in terms of unemployment compensation tax, cost of labor turnover, idle plant and equipment, and overtime payments during periods of peak production.

The employment stabilization coordinator can do much to bring about a closer cooperation between sales and production departments. At the Westinghouse Electric Corporation cooperation between manufacturing departments and sales and advertising departments stimulates sales at times when sales are needed to provide stabilized production and employment. Regularly scheduled meetings between department heads in staff and line departments can result in better planning of production, maintenance, purchasing, scheduling, and personnel activities.

In a company manufacturing fiber boxes, a planning manager was put on the staff of the plant superintendent. The planning manager's duties are to schedule the work of each machine and to work with a representative of the sales division in order to satisfy the requirements of customers with the least possible fluctuation in production and employment in the factory. In addition, this company issues to salesmen a weekly report informing them of the time required for normal delivery on various items.

Fairbanks, Morse and Company organized an unemployment department consisting of one man and two assistants whose sole duty is the elimination of unemployment among the company's workers. Each morning this department gets a report of the number of hours worked the preceding day by every employee. For each man who was not at work an investigation is made to determine whether the absence was voluntary or whether it was due to reasons for which the company might be responsible. A supervisor cannot lay off, discharge, or transfer a worker without clearing the matter with the unemployment department.

There is ample proof that a program of employment stabilization benefits both management and workers. If the program is soundly conceived and executed, it will produce greater stability in sales, production, and employment.

REFERENCES

American Legion. Employment Stabilization Service. *To Make Jobs More Steady and to Make More Steady Jobs.* St. Paul, Minn.: Webb Publishing Co., 1942. Various pagination.

Brower, F. Beatrice. *Annual Wage and Employment Guarantee Plans.* Studies in Personnel Policy No. 76. New York: National Industrial Conference Board, 1946. Pp. 55.

——. *Reducing Fluctuations in Employment; Experience in 31 Industries.* Studies in Personnel Policy No. 27. New York: National Industrial Conference Board, 1940. Pp. 60.

Chernick, Jack J. and George C. Hellickson. *Guaranteed Annual Wages.* Minneapolis: University of Minnesota Press, 1945. Pp. 146.

Dale, Ernest. *Annual Wages and Employment Stabilization Techniques.* Research Report No. 8. New York: American Management Association, 1945. Pp. 96.

Deupree, Richard R. "Management's Responsibility toward Stabilized Employment," in *Management Planning for Employment Stabilization.* General Management Series No. 135. New York: American Management Association, 1945. Pp. 3-9.

Latimer, Murray W. *Guaranteed Wages; Report to the President by the Advisory Board.* Washington: Government Printing Office, 1947. Pp. 473.

Myers, Charles A. *Economic Stabilization and the Wisconsin Act.* Employment Security Memorandum No. 10. Washington: U. S. Social Security Board, Employment Security Bureau, Research and Stabilization Division, 1940. Pp. 149. Processed.

Nielsen, Alice Lenore. *Guaranteed Employment and Annual Wage Plans.* Research and Statistics Report No. 25. Washington: National War Labor Board, Wage Stabilization Division, 1944. Pp. 37.

Snider, Joseph L. *The Guarantee of Work and Wages.* Cambridge, Mass.: Harvard University Graduate School of Business Administration, 1947. Pp. 191.

5

A Continuous High Level
of Employment in
Nonmanufacturing Activities

MANY TASKS which men in a simpler economy performed for themselves are done for us by people engaged in the service occupations—the barbers, shoe repairmen, taxi drivers, and so forth. The complexity of economic and social life creates a need for such specialists as statisticians, market analysts, and advertising men in addition to the established professions and service occupations. Since this specialization is efficient and convenient, service occupations have come to occupy an important place in the system of business enterprise. "Service occupations" will be used in this chapter to mean all non-manufacturing employment other than farming and mining. According to the National Resources Planning Board, more people are employed in service occupations than in industry and agriculture combined.

The level of employment in service occupations is dependent on the general economic level. If industrial workers suffer loss of income, the demand for services drops. During the postwar strikes in Detroit a dental supply company in that city lost one-third of its business. The explanation seemed to be that the demand for dental service had decreased because workers had lost income; and because the dentists had less work and less income they were doing more of their own laboratory work. In the same way, a low level of industrial activity will be reflected in curtailed business for barber shops, taxis, grocery stores, and other service establishments.

Although the level and stability of employment in nonmanufacturing occupations and professions will be influenced greatly by industrial conditions, there are several worthwhile efforts which may be made to maximize and stabilize service employment. Many of the proposals made in Chapter 3 with reference to industrial employment stabilization are applicable to nonmanufacturing establishments. These proposals will not be reviewed here, since it will be clear to the reader what modifications are necessary to adapt the industrial methods to service establishments. This chapter will deal with problems peculiar to employment in service establishments and occupations.

MAXIMIZING SERVICE EMPLOYMENT

Surveying the Community for Service Opportunities

Because of the importance of service occupations in creating jobs, each community should explore the service needs which exist. Service occupations exist to increase the efficiency of other businesses and individuals and to meet the welfare and service needs of the community. The chamber of commerce or board of trade might survey the service needs and opportunities of the community. The results of such a survey can be used in counseling those who wish to start a new business or expand an existing business. If the survey is used wisely, it will tend to prevent overcrowding in specific services and to provide needed additional services for the community. In determining service requirements it is often helpful to compare the number engaged in various services in the community with the number so engaged in other communities of similar size and activity. If, for example, it is found that in most communities of similar size and activity there is one beauty parlor for every six city blocks, while in the particular community being surveyed there is one for every twelve city blocks, it may be assumed that there are not enough beauty parlors to meet the demand or that there is a large untapped demand. Such a situation would indicate an opportunity for more beauty parlors. If, on the other hand, there are more beauty parlors than in the average community, this fact would discourage the establishment of more beauty parlors and would encourage present beauty parlors to broaden their services. For example, service might be extended to include massage and reducing treatments.

In its very nature, a service establishment renders services to individuals or businesses which no one individual or business alone would be able to support. An agricultural community may need canneries, frozen food lockers, and better marketing facilities. Another service need arises from the fact that small businesses cannot afford trained personnel in the fields of accounting, personnel administration, market analysis, and advertising. One organization, cooperatively supported, could supply counsel in these fields. Such service establishments increase efficiency and give employment by meeting real community needs. Emphasis should be placed on providing services not already available. Full employment will be achieved not by the displacement of one business by another but by expanding present businesses and by starting new businesses to meet real needs.

In *A Business of My Own,* Arthur Morgan lists 123 different opportunities for service enterprises. He describes this as a partial list which can be extended in any community. An equally stimulating booklet has been prepared by the Reader's Digest Association entitled *A Business of Your Own.* A large number of original ideas for new businesses are given along with some sound advice regarding the starting of a new business.

Factors Influencing the Success of a New Business

The specific factors influencing the success of a new business will vary with the type of business, but in general it would be unwise to start a new business until satisfactory answers have been given to the following questions:

1. Will the business meet a real need of the community?
2. Is a suitable location available?
3. Is there a satisfactory supply of materials and commodities?
4. Will it be possible to hire enough trained workers?
5. Can the business be soundly financed?
6. Does the person proposing to start the business have the necessary information, skill, character, and administrative ability?

It is not the purpose here to give detailed information regarding the methods of starting a new business. The Committee for Economic Development and the United States Department of Commerce have excellent materials on this subject. The series of booklets prepared by the United States Department of Commerce give specific recommendations regarding establishing and operating such businesses as a metal working shop, a shoe repair business, a sawmill, or a service station. By July, 1947, booklets had been prepared covering thirty-six different businesses.

In the local community, the man planning to start a new business can get much help from the banker, the lawyer, the chamber of commerce, and other businessmen. After the prospective businessman has read all the books, studied the community, sought sound advice, and evaluated his chances for success, he still must have the courage to accept some risk which is inherent in any new business venture.

Financing the New Business

Communities need to take steps to make available the funds required to finance new businesses. If the enterpriser wishing to start the business can offer collateral to secure a loan, he will have little difficulty in financing the venture. In most cases, however, the enterpriser must find an individual or an institution willing to share the risk of the venture to the extent of making an unsecured loan or accepting part ownership. The real need is for ways of establishing contact between individuals who wish to secure funds for new businesses and individuals or institutions that have funds to invest in such enterprises.

One solution to the problem of financing new businesses is the "equity fund," established by financial institutions that wish to pool a portion of their resources for the purpose of financing new businesses. The St. Louis Bank Credit Group is an example. Loans are made on a long-term, low-interest basis for the establishment of new businesses. Loans are made from an equity fund only after investigation has shown that the prospective borrower has integrity and ability as a businessman and that the proposed business will meet a need of the community or complement those businesses already established. In some cases, the interest rate is lower during the first years of the loan and rises later as the size of the loan decreases. Some equity funds make provision for a reduction of interest or payments in critical years.

Another solution to the problem of financing new businesses may be to establish an organization in the community whose sole purpose is to bring together investors and enterprisers seeking funds. This organization would do no more than serve as a clearinghouse or referral agency to facilitate contact between individuals who wish to secure funds to start new businesses and individuals who have money to invest in such enterprises. Since these investors would be making unsecured loans, they would really be accepting a stake in the business.

A third solution would be for a group of investors to pool the funds that they wish to invest in new businesses. This arrangement results in a sharing of the risks undertaken by the group. All the investors in such a group may wish to investigate and approve all enterprises financed by the group.

A final method of providing risk capital involves the establishment of a "development corporation" in which investors would purchase stock. Investments would then be made based on the judgment of the

board of directors of the corporation. This method would make it possible to use the funds of small investors who wish to share the risks and
rewards of investment in new business ventures but who do not have
the money, the management ability, or the inclination to start businesses of their own.

Increasing the Scope of Existing Services

Established service enterprises are often able to increase the scope
of their activities. This expansion of services often makes a more profitable business which benefits the business itself, its employees, and
the community.

An accounting firm might also offer calculating service and market
news. A bookstore might offer mimeograph service and employ a public stenographer. A farm feed store might employ an entomologist
and a soil expert. An automobile repair shop can extend its services
through a mobile repair unit. Valuable "by-products" of service establishments are often neglected just as industrial by-products are
often neglected. By-products may become a major source of income
for the service establishment as well as for the industrial plant.

Adaptation of Industrial Stabilization Methods

Businesses can be planned and managed to minimize seasonal fluctuations. Much of industry is at present geared to seasonal retail
sales. If through advertising, display, and price policies, retail sales
could be spaced evenly over the year, both the retail trade and industry would benefit. This is not easy because of consumers' habits.
Even though paint and wallpaper stores in many areas have carried
on extensive campaigns to induce the consumer to redecorate in
summer or winter, sales remain at a peak in the spring, because
spring is the accepted season for redecorating and cleaning. Only
gradually and by continual effort on the part of the retailer can
buying habits be changed.

Another answer to the problem of seasonal fluctuations is for one
business to combine goods and services that have their peak seasons in
different months. For example, a paint and wallpaper store might
carry a line of household gifts which would have a peak season from
October through December. Peak sales in decorating items would
occur from March through May; while during the summer outdoor
furniture and household goods could be featured. This method does,
of course, have the disadvantage of increasing inventories; and it
would require that the store devote less specialized attention to one

line of goods. Any attempt to minimize seasonal fluctuations in such a manner would have to be well planned, and the demand for the fill-in articles should be well established.

Other stabilization methods described in Chapter 3 which are directly applicable to service enterprises deal with sales policies, pricing, advertising, merchandising, and various procedures for selecting and training employees. Readers interested in any particular line of business can make their own adaptations. The report by the National Industrial Conference Board gives several examples of employment stabilization in nonmanufacturing establishments.[1]

The Responsibility of Financial Institutions

The financial institutions of a community can help to stabilize employment in service activities through the control of consumer credit and through the education of investors and borrowers.

To stabilize the local economy, credit should be made easier during periods of diminishing demand and more difficult during periods of increasing demand. Sound restrictions on installment buying will prevent overloading during boom periods and will spread purchases of goods and services over a period of time.

Financial institutions can perform a real service by encouraging people not to hoard their unspent income but to invest it in financial institutions where it will benefit both the investor and those who wish to borrow money for constructive purposes. Unless the income received during one period is either spent or put back into the income stream in the form of useful savings, there will be a curtailment of income during the next period. The consumer and, to some extent, the businessman can profit from information regarding expenditures and investments. Financial institutions must cooperate with schools and newspapers in this educational work.

Increasing Demand for Professional Services

The demand for professional services, as for all other goods and services, depends upon need and ability to pay. The need, furthermore, must be recognized by the prospective users of the service. The need for legal advice, for example, is often unrecognized and therefore is never translated into effective demand.

Education, which results in higher standards of living, will produce greater demand for professional services. To whatever extent professional ethics will permit, professional workers can acquaint the public

[1] F. Beatrice Brower, *Reducing Fluctuations in Employment*, pp. 49-52.

with the scope and value of their services. Lawyers might acquaint ordinary citizens with the services they have to offer in connection with such matters as wills, deeds, contracts, and taxes.

Another way to increase demand for professional services is to make it possible for people to pay for such services on the basis of insurance or annual payment plans. Hospitalization and surgical insurance has increased the demand for hospitalization and surgery by providing the means of payment.

In some communities it may be helpful to establish a clearinghouse for nurses and certain other professional workers. Through this clearinghouse people needing nursing service, for example, can contact available nurses.

Conclusions

There are several steps which citizens of a community can take to maximize and stabilize employment in nonmanufacturing activities. A survey of community needs usually will reveal a number of opportunities for businesses which, if properly administered and soundly financed, will contribute to the economic welfare of the community. Many needs can be met by an expansion of businesses already in operation.

Businessmen and all other citizens interested in community welfare must recognize that the goal is better business over a period of years rather than simply more business at a given time. The stabilization of business and service occupations can be achieved only through the joint efforts of consumers, businessmen, financial institutions, and workers in service occupations and professions. Better business for a community is a real challenge to cooperative effort.

REFERENCES

Colcord, Joanna C. *Your Community; Its Provision for Health, Education, Safety, and Welfare*. New York: Russell Sage Foundation, 1947. Pp. 263.

Colean, Miles L. *Stabilizing the Construction Industry*. Planning Pamphlet No. 41. Washington: National Planning Association, 1945. Pp. 38.

Committee for Economic Development. *Bank Credit; Your Postwar Program and Your Banker*. New York: The Committee, 1944. Pp. 17.

——. *Handbook for Retailers*. New York: The Committee, 1944. Pp. 25.

——. *Handbook for Wholesalers*. New York: The Committee, 1944. Pp. 34.

——. Committee on the Special Problems of Small Business. *Community Handbook on the Special Problems of Small Business*. New York: The Committee, 1945. Pp. 21.

——. ——. *Small Business after the War*. New York: The Committee, 1944. Pp. 15.

Leeper, Harry E. "Operations of Industrial Development Corporations," *Domestic Commerce*, XXXIV, No. 12 (December, 1946), 19–25.

Morgan, Arthur E. *A Business of My Own; Possibilities in Small Community Occupations and Industries*. Yellow Springs, Ohio: Community Service, Inc., 1946. Pp. 184.

Reader's Digest. *A Business of Your Own*. Pleasantville, N. Y.: Reader's Digest Association, Inc., 1946. Pp. 128.

Rosenthal, Richard Laurence. " ℞ for Smaller Business," *Harvard Business Review*, XXIV (1945), 22–31.

United States Bureau of Foreign and Domestic Commerce. *Veterans and Small Business* (articles). Washington: The Bureau, 1946. Pp. 63. Processed.

United States Department of Commerce. *Establishing and Operating Your Own Business*. Industrial Series No. 19. Washington: Government Printing Office, 1945. Pp. 30.

Wilhelm, Donald. *Credit Sources for Small Business*. U. S. Bureau of Foreign and Domestic Commerce, Economic (Small Business) Series No. 46. Washington: Government Printing Office, 1945. Pp. 34.

6

Agriculture and the Problem of Full Employment

Fʀᴏᴍ ᴀ ᴄᴏɴsɪᴅᴇʀᴀᴛɪᴏɴ of agriculture with respect to the problem of full employment, the most striking fact to emerge is that agriculture offers no opportunity for expansion in the total number of jobs available. The productivity of the average farm worker has been increasing for many years, and more rapidly than population has increased since 1910. Thus, although total farm production has increased throughout the years to keep pace with increases in total population, the number of workers required on farms has decreased steadily since 1910. And even though the ranks of farmers were somewhat depleted during the war years by farmers entering the armed forces or taking industrial jobs, it is believed that the number of persons still engaged in farming is large enough to supply the effective demand for farm products.

In view of the above observations, it is clear that there should be no "back to the land" movement. The popular notion that agriculture can absorb a large number of workers who cannot find industrial employment is not true. Those who have left farms for urban areas and industrial jobs should be encouraged to stay away from the farm. It follows also that veterans as a group should not be encouraged to farm. There will be a number of veterans, to be sure, whose knowledge of farming already equips them to become successful farmers; and retirements among older members of the present farmer group will provide some openings which could profitably be filled by such men. But, in general, veterans should not be encouraged to believe that there is much opportunity for them in farming.

It follows, finally, that subsistence farming should not be encouraged, either as a policy to care for otherwise unemployed persons or as a generalized "back to the farm" movement. As a matter of fact, there are already too many persons who are inadequately trained to

72

farm and who are farming land which is of marginal value for agricultural use. Such persons are literally underemployed, not in the sense that they do not have enough work to do, but in the sense that their efforts are relatively unproductive to themselves and therefore to society. The standard of living of many such farmers is extremely low, and their way of life gives rise to a "rural slum" that is just as undesirable to the nation as are slums in our urban areas. There is no opportunity for effective agricultural employment for these persons; and in terms of the goal of full employment the objective should be to provide business and industrial employment for them as well as for others who might consider subsistence farming as a means of livelihood.

RAISING and STABILIZING FARM INCOME

The interdependence of every element in our economy on every other element has been noted repeatedly throughout this book. The dependence of urban populations on the products of farms is of course obvious. In a less obvious but equally important way, urban areas depend upon rural citizens to purchase the goods and services produced by the city's businesses and industries. With over nine million members of the labor force engaged in agriculture, an unprosperous condition affecting farmers obviously cannot be tolerated if full employment is to be maintained.

The dependence of rural populations upon business and industrial prosperity is striking. The popular notion of the farmer as a self-sufficient individual is not true. Most farming, at least most successful farming, is a commercial venture which depends upon buying and selling for its existence. The farm is a "food factory," not a self-contained unit that produces only for the use of the farm family. Thus, although total farm production does not vary with changes in the business cycle, farm prices and therefore farm incomes are extremely sensitive to the ups and downs of the business cycle. According to Schultz:[1]

When business became prosperous and boomed, farm income rose fully twice as fast as nonfarm income; when business slumped and became depressed, the income of farm people from farming fell more precipitously and decidedly further than the income of persons not on farms. Between business fluctuations and wars, farm income derived from the sales of crops and livestock is occasionally very very good; as frequently it is very very bad. And the going from good to bad is not what makes farm life interesting.

[1]Theodore W. Schultz, *Agriculture in an Unstable Economy* (New York: McGraw-Hill Book Co., 1945), pp. 214-16.

In view of the declining need for agricultural workers and in view of the striking interdependence of urban and rural populations, it will be clear that, from the standpoint of the problem of full employment, the agricultural problem revolves almost entirely around procedures for maintaining a high level of farm income and reducing the sharp fluctuations to which that income level has been subjected in the past. It is not within the province of this book to describe measures of a primarily national character which are intended to solve the problems of agricultural employment. The measures to be suggested represent those which can be taken by farm groups or urban groups at the community level in an attempt to increase the general level of farm income and to minimize fluctuations.

Industrial and Business Success

The foremost measure that merits attention as a means of achieving a high and stable level of farm income is the achievement of a high and stable level of business and industrial employment. According to Schultz,[2] "If the total of nonagricultural production were to become as full and as regular as the over-all agricultural production has been, most of the instability in farm income associated with business fluctuations would be eliminated."

Although Schultz is referring primarily to agricultural problems from the national standpoint and to the achievement of business and industrial stability at the national level, the importance of local business and industrial success in determining the degree of success of farmers in the neighboring territory cannot be overlooked. Insofar as urban and rural areas can be integrated into a more or less self-sufficient community, the importance of local business and industrial success in raising and stabilizing farm incomes will become even greater.

Retirement of Submarginal Land

A second measure calculated to increase and stabilize levels of farm income involves the elimination of the "rural slum." It has been pointed out that one of the main reasons for the rural slum is the attempt to farm land that is not suitable for agricultural use. The remedy for this situation lies in the provision of industrial and business opportunities for persons who are now operating subsistence farms, and in procedures for inducing such persons to accept industrial employment. Leadership toward the attainment of this objective can be given both by urban groups and by farm associations.

[2]*Ibid.*, p. 219.

Improvement in Methods of Farming

The improvement of farming methods may be considered as a third means of increasing and stabilizing farm incomes. This is a matter to which attention has been devoted for many years by the United States Department of Agriculture and by the agricultural colleges of the country. The productivity of the average farm worker has increased sharply during the past thirty years, and much of that improvement in productivity stems from the efforts of the organizations just mentioned. Although further research will undoubtedly continue to be profitable, the major hope for improvement appears to lie in bringing about a wider understanding and acceptance by farmers of information which is already available on farming methods. In any farming locality striking differences can be noticed in the productivity of adjacent farms, differences almost solely attributable to variations in the knowledge and the skill of farm operators. Although it is not within the province of this book to treat farming methods as such, it may be helpful to enumerate some types of improved methods which bear upon the problem of higher and more stable income on the farm.

Land Conservation. The long-term deterioration of farm lands in many regions through improper use of the land has proceeded to the point where it is a national tragedy and a source of disaster for the regions directly affected. The dust bowl of the Southwest offers a striking example of such tragic misuse of the land. Deterioration of the land in some southern states is a matter of common knowledge, and its effect upon the health and economic welfare of the population in those areas is appalling. Misuse of the land is causing deterioration also in the fertile plains states.

It is a matter of the utmost importance to the communities of America to exercise vigilance with respect to the continued productivity of their agricultural resources. This is a matter which should engage the attention of both urban and rural groups.

Selection of Crops. Prominent among the hazards of farming are the risks of unfavorable weather and of plant and animal diseases. Much is already known about weather-resistant and disease-resistant varieties of many crops, disease-resistant breeds of livestock, and the use of insecticides, vaccines, and other preventive measures. At present, many farmers do not make use of this information; and the wider application of such information could do much to reduce the hazards of agriculture.

The selection of crops merits attention also as a means of hedging against the hazards of price fluctuation. And finally, the selection of farm products deserves consideration with respect to the opportunities that will be provided for year-round employment on the farm. Some farm products require considerable labor during a short portion of the year and offer very little productive use of time for the farmer during other periods of the year. On the other hand, livestock and dairy operations, for example, afford year-round employment.

COOPERATION AMONG FARMERS

A farm which can be operated efficiently by one man or one family is not large enough to make use of many of the devices of large-scale production which have proved advantageous to operators of large farms. Many of these advantages, however, can be obtained by cooperative effort on the part of a number of individual farmers in a given neighborhood. The types of cooperative effort which are to be mentioned are not new, but these procedures have not been tried out fully in many communities where they may be applicable.

Use of Equipment

The cooperative ownership of threshing equipment has been common for many years. By extension of the principle of cooperative ownership of equipment, there is little doubt that many of the advantages of mechanization and large-scale operation could be obtained for the individual owner of a small farm. Cooperative rental of airplane services for the spraying of crops and livestock affords a current illustration of possibilities.

The Sharing of Labor

The exchange of labor among neighboring farmers during the threshing season is a custom of long standing. It is also common for farmers to get together to erect barns and other farm buildings. Although the principle is not new, the possibilities of labor pooling as a means of attaining more efficient production deserve systematic exploration.

Cooperative Buying and Selling

When farmers pool their orders for such supplies as feed, seed, and fertilizer, it becomes possible for them to obtain the advantage of the lower prices associated with quantity orders. There are many instances of the extension of this principle of cooperative buying to furniture, hardware, clothing, and groceries through the formation of the "farm co-op" store. Against the possible advantages of such activities on the part of farm groups there must be placed the disadvantage that such operations may require the farmer to devote attention to problems other than farming. The possibilities involved in such cooperative effort nevertheless warrant serious consideration by farm groups in each community.

As in the case of cooperative buying, group effort in the sale of farm products often proves to be of value. Cooperatively owned grain elevators, for example, have proved profitable in many communities.

URBAN-RURAL COORDINATION AT THE COMMUNITY LEVEL

Self-sufficiency of a Community

The attainment of self-sufficiency is not a reasonable objective for a family, a community, or a nation. Our present high standard of living results in large part from the development of specialization. The average American community cannot produce its own motor cars, clothing, sugar, or tea as economically as these items can be produced in centers which are naturally suited to such production or in which efficient productive facilities have been developed. Thus, the development of community self-sufficiency in any ultimate sense is not recommended.

It is suggested, however, that community self-sufficiency be carried as far as it is economically feasible to do so. There are many activities for which a given community is exceptionally well suited, and which are not carried on simply because no one happens to have undertaken them. There are other activities which, though a particular community may have no peculiarly advantageous position with respect to them, can be just as easily carried on in that community as anywhere else. With respect to such activities, there seems to be some advantage in having each community extend its functions as widely as possible. Problems of all sorts can be solved more easily if they occur at the community level than if they occur at more remote points. The problems are recognized more quickly, understood more fully, and solved more effectively because the persons involved in the solution can have face-to-face contact with each other. Insofar as problems can be kept at the community level, the prospect for rapid readjustment to changing conditions is increased; and the danger of the spread of boom or depression throughout the entire economy is thus reduced.

It is with a view to obtaining that desired degree of flexibility that the following suggestions are offered as ways of integrating the urban and rural elements of a community.

The Production of Edible Farm Products for Local Consumption

It is common in many communities to find some items of food being brought in from points many hundreds of miles away which could just as economically be produced by farmers in the surrounding area. It would be economically sound to produce such products in the local area; and the development of local production would have the further advantage of keeping the problem of coordinating production and consumption at the local level. The reduction in costs of distribution would benefit both producers and consumers.

The Production of Farm Products for Local Industrial Use

Although industry still utilizes only a relatively small proportion of total farm output, the selection of crops which can be used in nearby industrial plants merits serious consideration by farmers. And just as it is desirable for the farmer to consider the production of commodities which can be utilized locally for industrial purposes, so it is important for industries to consider locating in communities where their raw material needs can be supplied by local agriculture.

Local Storage and Processing Facilities

The development of industries for the processing of local food products or for offering service to the local producers of food has proceeded by no means as far as it might in many communities. For example, in areas devoted to the growing of perishable products, local cold storage plants may be profitable. Quick-freeze plants or canning factories may also be located in such communities. In livestock producing areas, a local packing plant may be advantageous to the community. In dairy sections, a cheese factory may represent a profitable business venture. While these illustrations seem obvious, such activities do not exist in many communities where they would be profitable. Habit and chance often dictate the economic activities of a community, rather than thoughtful planning.

Industrial Use of Farm Labor during Slack Seasons

In many farming communities, there seems to be no escape from the fact that a great deal of work has to be done on the farms during the growing season, whereas there is little to do during the winter months. As a means of increasing the income of rural groups, consideration should be given to the establishment of industries in the urban communities which can concentrate their production during the winter months and make use of farm labor during the farmers' slack season. Such a program offers not only a method of increasing the income of farm groups, but also a way of adding some industrial activity in a community which has already absorbed all the labor which is available on a year-round basis.

The fact that such utilization of farm labor in industrial occupations has not already been made to any considerable extent probably indicates that such a procedure poses serious problems to the management of an industry which attempts to do so. One such problem is the reluctance of farmers to accept urban employment during the winter months. Educational procedures, which might be sponsored by both urban and rural groups, are needed in order to increase the occupational mobility of rural people.

A second problem in providing such employment for farm people arises from the reluctance of industrial managers to employ part-time help of any sort unless it is necessary to do so. The productive efficiency of part-time workers is usually considerably less than that of full-time employees. They have less motivation to work hard and get ahead, whether they be farmers, housewives, or students, because they have other objectives which absorb a considerable part of their energy and interest. Turnover and absenteeism are greater among part-time employees; and because of transportation problems and the occasional odd jobs that need to be done around a farm in the wintertime, turnover and absenteeism might be expected to be particularly high among farmers. Finally, the business which attempts to draw much of its help from the farmer group during the winter is thereby confined to winter operations; and thus it lacks the economy and flexibility associated with year-round operation.

It follows from an enumeration of these problems that few industrial managers are likely to consider operating with a substantial number of part-time employees unless employment levels are so high that help is hard to get. Nevertheless, the idea might be tried out by some interested groups as a community experiment. The problem involved is important. The underutilization of farm labor during the winter months coupled with the generally unsatisfactory income level of farm groups makes it urgent for leaders in urban-rural areas to attempt to provide off-season industrial employment for these persons if it is possible to do so.

Education in Agriculture

Communities can be found, even in predominantly agricultural areas of the country, where the schools offer little or no training in agriculture. This is true despite the fact that the young people from the surrounding farms get their education in the city schools. Those who return to the farm without going on to agricultural college have no opportunity to learn how to improve the efficiency of their farming operations unless they are taught how to do so in the local schools. Studies of the need for this type of education should be made by the school administration in every urban-rural area.

Provision for the Educational, Physical, and
  Recreational Needs of Farm Youth

It is recognized that the birth rate among urban populations is usually so low that such populations would be rapidly depleted if people did not come into the cities from other areas; whereas the birth rate among rural groups is considerably above the level necessary to maintain the population of the rural areas. This means that business and industry look to the farm for their new employees and that cities draw their future citizens from rural areas. Aside from the element of parental affection, rural people actually have less of a stake in the health, well-being, and citizenship of farm youth than do city people. Yet the cost of rearing and educating the youth of the nation is now being borne to a disproportionate extent by the farming group. It is thus realistic rather than philanthropic for urban areas to share the cost of providing education, medical service, and recreation for the children of farm people. If farm youth prove to any extent to be difficult to employ in industry by reason of defects in health, personality, or training, the loss to industry and society is considerable. The leaders of both urban and rural groups should give consideration to the development of the young people of the surrounding farm community.

REFERENCES

Aull, G. H. and J. M. Stepp. *The Postwar Economic Outlook in an Agricultural-Industrial Area.* Bulletin No. 355. Clemson: South Carolina Agricultural Experiment Station of Clemson Agricultural College, 1945. Pp. 43.

Benedict, Murray R. *A Retirement System for Farmers.* Planning Pamphlet No. 49. Washington: National Planning Association, 1946. Pp. 43.

Beveridge, William H. *Full Employment in a Free Society*. New York: W. W. Norton and Co., 1945. Pp. 429.

Burchfield, Laverne. *Our Rural Communities: A Guidebook to Published Materials on Rural Problems*. Chicago: Public Administration Service, 1947. Pp. 201.

Fleddérus, Mary and Mary Van Kleeck. *Technology and Livelihood; An Inquiry into the Changing Technological Basis for Production as Affecting Employment and Living Standards*. New York: Russell Sage Foundation, 1944. Pp. 237.

Friends Service, Inc. *Penn-Craft in Progress*. Philadelphia: American Friends Service Committee. 24 unnumbered pp.

Schultz, Theodore W. *Agriculture in an Unstable Economy*. New York: McGraw-Hill Book Co., 1945. Pp. 299.

United States Bureau of Agricultural Economics. *Changing Employment in Agriculture*. Washington: Government Printing Office, 1945. Pp. 19.

——. *Technology on the Farm: A Special Report by an Interbureau Committee and the Bureau of Agricultural Economics*. Washington: Government Printing Office, 1940. Pp. 224.

United States National Resources Committee. Science Committee. *Technological Trends and National Policy, Including the Social Implication of New Inventions, June, 1937. Report of the Subcommittee on Technology to the National Resources Committee*. (75th Congress, 1st Session, House Document 360.) Washington: Government Printing Office, 1937. Pp. 388.

Wallace, Henry A. *Sixty Million Jobs*. New York: Reynal & Hitchcock, Simon & Schuster, 1945. Pp. 216.

7

Labor Organizations and Full Employment

It has been pointed out throughout this book that the dependence of every group in our economy upon every other group is perhaps the most striking factor to be reckoned with in the search for continued prosperity and full employment. If the interests of laboring groups are seriously jeopardized, then investors, business and industrial managements, and the consuming public cannot long remain unaffected. On the other hand, if the position of investors or business and industrial managers is endangered, then any apparent advantage to laboring groups will be only temporary.

All groups within the nation and within each community must be concerned with the problem of full employment. There is no group, however, which is more directly affected by the level of employment than the workers themselves. It is thus of the utmost importance that workers, largely through the policies and practices of their organizations, take a serious interest in pursuing those objectives which will lead us toward the goal of continued full employment. In proposing certain policies and practices for the consideration of labor groups, we do not mean to imply that the present practices of labor groups are often found to violate these principles, any more than to imply that local governments or businesses and industries are generally pursuing policies at variance with the principles outlined earlier in the book. But if the objective is to be attained, all groups—local government, businesses and industries, labor, and others—must consistently and intensively work toward that goal by all possible means.

LABOR POLICIES

Labor's Stake in the Soundness of the Business

When we turn from the national scene, with all its complex relationships of one group to another, to the community scene, which is the point of emphasis in this book, it becomes apparent that the employees of any particular company have a great stake in the continued stability and good competitive position of the establishment in which they work. If it is assumed that the community is roughly "in balance," in the sense that there are enough jobs in the community for all who wish to work and enough people to do all of the work in the community, then the failure of a particular enterprise, or even a temporary setback in the business, will inevitably work a serious hardship upon its employees. At best, they are faced with a period of temporary idleness and loss of income; at worst they may face the necessity of uprooting themselves from their home town and moving elsewhere in search of work. Laboring groups have just as much of a stake in the continued soundness of the business as have the investors in that business or its management group. It follows that, while laboring groups will naturally want to be vigilant in the protection and promotion of their own immediate interests, such as good working conditions and good wages, they should be just as vigilant as the board of directors or the management in working toward the continued success of the enterprise. Some of the ways in which laboring groups can protect their stake in the business are given in the following pages.

Profits as an Essential Element of the Free Enterprise System

It is necessary to recognize that people will not put money into the buildings and equipment that are essential to provide jobs unless there is a reasonable likelihood that they will find it profitable to do so. No one ever invests money for the primary purpose of providing a job for someone else; he invests money simply because he believes it will be profitable to do so. This is equally true of the man who has twenty-five dollars to invest and of the man who has twenty-five million dollars to invest. The employment resulting from the development of new businesses and the expansion of old businesses depends entirely upon the creation of conditions which will lead investors to believe that it will be profitable for them to invest their money in such undertakings. Labor's stake in the creation and maintenance of a favorable situation for profit seekers is therefore enormous. Any policy or practice on the part of labor organizations which jeopardizes profits of the business in which their members are employed can be disastrous to the opportunity of those members for employment.

Stability in the Rules of the Game

When a potential investor considers the establishment or expansion of a business which would provide jobs for people, he must weigh the possible profits from his investment against the risks which he is taking in making that particular investment. A new risk, arising from the increasing power of labor organizations, is the uncertainty as to the attitude which the unions representing his employees will take toward the continued success of the business. It is obvious to the potential investor that if his employees are well organized so that they present a united front on any issue, they have it in their power to bankrupt the enterprise. The prospective investor therefore needs to know whether it is likely that the organization of his employees will take that point of view or whether they will be interested, as he is, in the continued success of the business. It is suggested, therefore, that labor groups within each community review their policies and practices in order to develop a consistent point of view upon which prospective investors in business ventures can count.

One of the important elements of stability in the rules of the game, which might be reviewed, is the attitude of the labor organization toward observance of the labor contract throughout its duration. If the prospective investor must face the risk of nonobservance of the contract, he will be deterred from making investments which would provide jobs.

Full Production

It has often been pointed out that a good standard of living depends basically upon our capacity as a nation to produce a large enough "stock pile" of goods and services so that each person's share in that stock pile will be large enough to constitute a good standard of living. While this is undoubtedly true, this fact has not been sufficient in most cases to convince the employees of a particular company of the desirability of maximum production on the part of each individual. Employees often believe that if they "slow down" on their individual jobs, they will thereby make their jobs last, and that the slowdown will thus result in full employment for them as individuals. Workers sometimes believe also that by opposing the introduction of laborsaving machinery and improved production methods, the employees of a particular company may assure their own continued employment, even though it is at the expense of the consumers of their product who are thereby forced to pay higher prices.

Actually, decreased productivity of workers causes higher prices for the product; higher prices reduce demand for the product; and the final result is that fewer workers are needed. If a company fails to maintain its competitive position its very existence is threatened, and the slowdown that was to preserve jobs may result in loss of employment for all workers in the company.

For other reasons also, workers will benefit from unrestricted production. The value of the company's product will determine many things of importance to labor such as the amount of money available for distribution as wages for workers and as dividends for the owners of the business, and the amount of money that can be spent on employee benefits and improved working conditions. If the company is to continue to operate, wages and other benefits to workers are strictly limited by the value of the goods produced.

Wage Levels

In a free country the relationships that must exist among prices, profits, and wages are so sensitive that no one of these factors can be looked at without considering each of the other two. If profit expectations are not sufficiently high, people will not choose to invest their money in those business enterprises that might have provided jobs. If prices are not properly adjusted, people cannot buy the products of a particular business in sufficient quantity to enable that business to continue. Finally, if wages are too low, wage earners cannot buy the commodities which they and others have made. Low wages may lead in turn to low levels of consumption, production, and employment.

There is, in contrast to this point of view, a commonly stated belief that an increase in wage levels will increase purchasing power and will therefore tend to bring about a higher level of prosperity and employment. In the light of the above stated relationships among prices, profits, and wages, it is questionable whether in any given instance a rise in wage levels will lead toward this desired result. If the rise in wage levels should result in a total absorption of profits, then the business may go bankrupt; and the result will thus be not fuller employment for the employees of that enterprise, but no employment at all. If, on the other hand, prices of the product are increased in order to maintain adequate profit levels, then the commodity may be priced higher than its potential purchasers can pay or higher than competitive products, and the result may again be a serious cutback or bankruptcy for the company.

It is not within the province of this book to propose an adequate wage policy for the consideration of labor organizations. It is intended only to point out that the wage policy of labor organizations must take account of labor's enormous stake in the continued success of the enterprises that furnish employment and must recognize the relationships among prices, wages, and profits.

LABOR PROGRAMS

Employment Stabilization and Expansion

Employee and management groups certainly meet on common ground in activities to promote the success of the business. Both management and labor have an interest in, and responsibility for, sound programs to expand and stabilize employment. Management and labor can cooperate in carrying out the programs described in Chapter 3. The contributions of labor include a willingness to accept technological changes, plant-wide seniority to allow flexibility in transfers, and cooperation in maintaining high productivity. Cooperation in these ways is the price that labor must pay for increased security of employment.

Training

Full employment cannot be taken to mean that all persons can continue to work indefinitely in the same occupation. Persons in many occupations such as that of buggy maker have, at one period or other, faced the necessity of learning new occupations. The ranks of candlemakers must have been reduced by the introduction of kerosene lamps; and the ranks of telegraph operators were similarly reduced with the advent of telephone, teletype, and radio communication. Labor organizations should certainly have an interest in the development of training programs to facilitate the entry of workers into new occupations, rather than in "feather-bedding" practices and other procedures for the restriction of production. The promotion of training programs offers a fertile field for the activity of local unions, company by company and community by community, as a way of meeting the problems of declining opportunity for employment in particular occupations.

A Community Climate Favorable to Business Enterprise

Technological change affects not only individual occupations but also whole lines of products and even the success of entire companies. In any community, even in normal times, many establishments go out of business every year; and with every business which thus disappears a number of jobs are lost in the community. This loss will be made up in the community only if someone chooses to start a new enterprise or expand an old business in that community.

It is well known that companies that are searching for new locations for their business operations attach great significance to the attitudes of employees and labor organizations in each community under consideration. It is not uncommon for established enterprises to move at considerable expense from a community in which the attitude of labor organizations is not favorable toward the continuance of their business into a community which appears to be more receptive. Thus, a community which is not favorable toward the continuance of profitable business and industrial operations is likely to face a gradual reduction of employment opportunity which, over a period of five or ten years, may damage the community beyond repair as a place in which employees can live a full and prosperous life. The stake of labor organizations in maintaining a community climate which is favorable toward the prosperity of business enterprise is just as great as the stake of any other group within the community.

It is not intended at this time to consider whether labor or management groups are more responsible for the existence of poor labor-management relationships in a community. It is intended only to point out that every group in the community will benefit from seeing to it that such conditions do not prevail locally.

Educational Programs for Members of Labor Organizations

Some policies and programs have been suggested in previous sections which promise to further the long-term interest of labor organizations in an increased level of prosperity and full employment for their members. These policies and programs have been contrasted with other points of view, which, while they may appear to be to the immediate advantage of laboring groups, may ultimately defeat the objective which they were intended to attain. It is recognized that in any democratic organization, whether it be a labor organization, a luncheon club, a city, or a nation, policies and programs cannot be effectively carried out unless they meet with the approval of the membership. It is thus necessary for the leaders of labor organizations in each community not only to determine policies which will actually lead toward the fulfillment of their objectives but also to educate their members to a recognition of the essential rightness of those policies and programs. As an example of a principle that must be explained through a good program of labor education, the basic point of this chapter may be mentioned; namely, that the members of labor organizations have just as great a stake in the success of local business enterprises as do the boards of directors, stockholders, and management members of those enterprises. This basic point is not always recognized by the members of labor organizations, just as the general dependence of all groups in the community upon one another is not always recognized by other groups in the community. The responsibility of local labor leaders to take the initiative in developing educational programs for their members is of the utmost importance.

Security Programs

Considerable progress has been made since the early thirties in the development of security programs that are designed to spread the risks of certain misfortunes against which each individual employee cannot afford to protect himself. Unemployment compensation programs, old-age and survivors' pensions, and death benefits are now available for many members of the working population, as are many special forms of assistance to handicapped persons which had not formerly been provided. There is little doubt as to the desirability of such security programs, insofar as they can be soundly financed, because of the extent to which they free individuals from the fear of unavoidable hazards. Such programs are naturally a matter of concern to individual employees and to labor organizations. Some of the directions which their efforts may take in the promotion of such programs are indicated below.

Uniformity of Application. Particularly with respect to unemployment compensation procedures, there is great variation in the programs from state to state. The efforts of labor organizations might well be devoted toward improvements in the provisions of these programs in many states and in the administration of the laws.

Extension of Coverage of Present Programs. Present programs, particularly the old-age and survivorship provisions of the Social Security Act, fail to cover many groups of persons whose need of such security is just as great as the need of those now covered.

Promotion of Additional Security Programs. Hospital and medical services, for example, are at present provided only by certain individual organizations. The efforts of labor organizations might be helpful in working out sound programs on a broader basis and in promoting the adoption of such plans.

Company versus National Security Programs. Many individual companies now operate such security programs as payment for absence due to illness, hospital and medical services, pensions, and death benefits. Insofar as such programs depend on contributions from the company, it is clear that the extent to which employees may benefit from such programs depends upon the attitude of the management of each individual company and upon the financial capacity of that company to provide such benefits. It is an open question whether ultimately such programs should be the responsibility of individual companies or whether all such security programs should be administered by the government in order that all working groups may benefit from them regardless of the policies and fortunes of the particular company in which they happen to be employed. The careful study of security programs and the promotion of sound programs in line with the results of such studies should represent a useful field of activity for labor organizations.

CONCLUSION

It may be emphasized again that the problems that are confronted in working toward the achievement and maintenance of a high level of employment are extremely complex, and that the best thinking of all groups in each community will be necessary if the objective is to be attained. There is perhaps no domestic issue which affects so directly the fortunes of employee groups as this problem of full employment. It is to be hoped that the problem will engage the increasing attention of employee groups and the leaders of their organizations.

REFERENCES

Bye, Raymond T. and William W. Hewett. *Applied Economics.* New York: F. S. Crofts & Co., 1946. Pp. 690.

Frey, John P. "Labor's Stake in Capitalism," *Nation's Business,* XXXI (September, 1943), 27, 70ff.

Hall, Helen. (Mrs. Paul Underwood Kellogg.) "Empty Pay Envelopes, and Peace," *Survey Graphic,* XXXIV (1945), 394–96.

Hillman, Sidney. "Labor and Employment Planning," *Survey Graphic,* XXXII (1943), 174-75.

Johnston, Eric A. *A Warning to Labor—And to Management.* Washington: Chamber of Commerce of the United States, 1944. Pp. 13.

Lester, Richard A. *Providing for Unemployed Workers in the Transition.* New York: McGraw-Hill Book Co., 1945. Pp. 152.

Murray, Philip. *C.I.O. Re-employment Plan*. Publication No. 116. Washington: C.I.O. Department of Research and Education, n.d. Pp. 29.

——. "An Economic Bill of Rights," *Survey Graphic*, XXXIV (1945), 397–99ff.

Slichter, Sumner. "Responsibility of Organized Labor for Employment," *American Economic Review*, XXXV (1945), 193–208.

"Vital Issues Facing Unions: Shift in Views of Leaders; What AFL Delegates Think of Wage, Employment, Political Problems," *United State News*, XV (October 15, 1943), 27–30.

Woll, Matthew. *Steps Necessary for High Post-War Employment*. Washington: American Federation of Labor, 1943. Pp. 11.

8

The Contribution of Community Planning to Full Employment

IT SHOULD perhaps be emphasized again that this book is not written primarily about local planning, but rather about the things which individual citizens or local organizations can do to achieve and maintain a high level of employment. Thus, industrial stabilization methods or agricultural cooperative ventures, which are not ordinarily a part of books on local planning, are essential topics in this book. On the other hand, the kinds of public buildings which the community should have and their location are topics which are covered in a book on city planning, but they are only of borderline interest in the present context.

While there are differences between a community program for full employment and local planning in the technical sense, these differences are overshadowed by the complementary nature of the two kinds of programs. Modern community planning, for example, is much broader than the "city beautiful" concept of a generation ago. Many city planners recognize the importance of a study of the local economic structure in making plans for the physical and social development of the community. Such a study is also basic in a program for full employment. Differences in detail and in emphasis reflect differences in the specific objectives of the programs but not in their general aim, which is to provide a better community in which to work and live.

Physical and social planning is related to planning for full employment from the standpoint of a setting or "community climate" for the economic life of the community. Local regulations affecting industry and business may discourage expansion or the location of new industries. Property taxes may be too high. Inadequate housing facilities may not attract enough skilled laborers to supply the needs of industry. Similarly, inadequate provisions for health protection, education, and recreation may discourage workers and industrial organizations from locating in the community. Factors such as these may affect the daily operations of a business or industry as well as its long-term prospects for continuous and profitable operation. These are some of the topics included in a book on community planning.

The extent to which local plans provide a sound setting for economic development and the measures that are proposed in these plans for a community's economic development are areas under consideration in this chapter. The principal planning organizations found in most communities will be described briefly in the next section. Following this, examples of different kinds of plans will be given. These examples include: (1) plans for business and industrial progress; (2) plans for public works and the improvement of public services; and (3) comprehensive city plans. The last part of this chapter deals with the important factors involved in sound community planning.

PLANNING ORGANIZATIONS AT THE LOCAL LEVEL

The principal organizations which have sponsored plans for community development are: (a) the Committee for Economic Development, (b) local chambers of commerce, (c) civic boards, and (d) local governments. In addition there are other organizations interested in stimulating local action and thinking toward specific or broad economic objectives. Among them are newspapers, banks, social groups, industries, and business and industrial associations.

Committee for Economic Development

The Committee for Economic Development is a national organization supported by private industries and "organized to assist commerce and industry to make its maximum contribution toward maintaining high levels of productivity and employment in the postwar period." The Committee has had two divisions: a research division and a field development division. The latter, which has been discontinued, functioned at local levels through local committees made up of business, industrial, and civic leaders who stimulated and encouraged planning by individual companies. The field development division planned to have a local committee in every city with a population of 10,000 or more. At the end of the war there were approximately 3,000 local committees. In general, the work of local committees was directed toward combating the spirit of defeatism, which was anticipated as a postwar phenomenon, by stimulating businessmen to appraise their postwar prospects and to do something about them.

Chambers of Commerce

There are approximately 1,700 local chambers affiliated with the Chamber of Commerce of the United States. In addition, there are a number of local chambers without such national affiliation. Members of the local organizations support national policies and measures formulated by the Chamber of Commerce of the United States, and also formulate and support plans at the community level. Almost all local chambers in communities above 3,000 population were active in making postwar plans.

These plans center around the business and industrial problems with which members of the local chamber are most concerned, or they may also include the interests of other segments of the community.

Civic Boards

Civic boards composed of public-minded citizens may organize in response to local needs and problems when the need for planning is not being met in other ways. A good example of such action is the Louisville Area Development Association, a nonprofit civic corporation. Its membership includes the mayor and representatives from local industries, newspapers, and labor organizations. It is financed jointly by industry, business, local government, and labor. The objectives are "to correct faults that have resulted from Louisville's haphazard growth, to create an orderly framework for the more prosperous and progressive city Louisville can become, and to safeguard the enormous industrial expansion the war years have brought to Louisville."

In Louisville there is also an official public planning agency, the Louisville and Jefferson County Planning and Zoning Commission. Some members of the public agency also serve on the Louisville Area Development Association. The official agency is primarily concerned with problems of zoning and does not have the time, the facilities, or the finances to undertake the projects which have been sponsored by the Louisville Area Development Association.

Local Governments

Almost all states have passed enabling legislation for the creation of city and county planning boards. In cities that have created a planning commission, the activities of the planning commission may be limited to physical planning, zoning, and building ordinances, or they may include comprehensive planning for the community. These public plans are closely tied up with state plans administratively, legally, and financially.

PLANS FOR BUSINESS AND INDUSTRIAL PROGRESS

Most of the published reports on city plans deal with programs for business and industrial progress. Many of these do not warrant consideration as plans inasmuch as no specific objectives are indicated and no course of action is considered. Some of them are surveys of opinions or facts about a particular aspect of the local economy. Others are promotional in nature, having a few facts and perhaps a great deal of unwarranted enthusiasm for a "bigger and better" city. During the war there were, in addition, a number of "work pile" plans. The work pile included all of the alterations, repairs, and new construction work that merchants, industrial firms, and homeowners in a community planned to undertake during the transition from a wartime to a peacetime economy. The size of the work pile was measured by the total number of dollars required to complete this deferred work.

The report which is described below is more appropriately considered a plan from the standpoint of criteria to be discussed in a later section.

"A City Looks at Itself"

This report was prepared by the Spartanburg, South Carolina, Chamber of Commerce. A study was made of the city and county of Spartanburg, and each of nine postwar planning committees undertook a study of some aspect of community life and prepared a factual report of resources and problems in each area. Recommendations for action were made by each committee.

The scope of this plan can be indicated to some degree by noting the committees which participated in the study—agriculture and marketing, aviation, education, finance, industrial expansion, public building, roads and streets, public health, social improvements, and utilities. The report of the Committee on Industrial Expansion is described in some detail as an example of what each committee did.

The introduction to the report on industrial expansion points out the changing character of the economic structure. At one time a purely agricultural county, Spartanburg now produces manufactured products which exceed its agricultural products in value. A favorable climate, an adequate labor supply, excellent railroad facilities, and an adequate water supply have made possible the industrial development which has taken place in the county.

A study of the types of industries located in the county shows that, while textile manufacturing is the dominant industry, Spartanburg has many other kinds of industries. A creosoting plant, a textile machinery plant, and a grain and feed mill, which are among the larger nontextile industries, export their products extensively outside the county and the state.

A study of the mortality rate of new industries which located in Spartanburg between January, 1923, and July, 1942, shows that out of 83 new industries chartered 42 or 50.6 per cent have survived. The survival rate is higher than it is for three other counties in the state which chartered a larger number of new industries in the same period.

Employment data taken from the 1940 census are presented by occupations and by sex. Additional information is given on the present and anticipated levels of employment. This information was obtained in 1944 by a questionnaire sent to a number of local manufacturers.

Since textile manufacture is the dominant industry in the county, employing four-fifths of the industrial workers in the county, the types of products manufactured in the mills and the textile supplies used in the mills are considered in some detail.

Some of the problems which this committee considered are the freight rate for coal, which places South Carolina cities at a disadvantage compared with cities in some adjoining states, and the inadequate storage facilities in the city resulting from an excessive licensing fee for warehouses. As a result of its study the Committee on Industrial Expansion made a number of recommendations which include:

1. The establishment of at least three warehouse terminals at different points in the city.

2. The reduction of the present license fee for wholesale and retail storage warehouses in order that local industries can compete with firms in other southern cities.

3. The encouragement of new industries to locate in the community, particularly those which can be financed with local capital.

4. A list of industries which could operate profitably in the city and county of Spartanburg.

5. A suggestion that tax assessments be made on the basis of actual

value, thus greatly reducing the tax rate without reducing tax revenues. The committee felt that the present basis of assessment discourages investors and industrialists.

6. Improvement of the city in several respects through the efforts of the city government and local industries. It is pointed out that many operators of small businesses are influenced in the selection of a city by its appearance.

The last section of the report gives an over-all summary and raises many questions regarding the means of implementing the many recommendations. While the report omits some studies that are basic to planning (for example, a study of population trends and estimates of population in the future) it nevertheless ranks high among plans of this type.

PLANS FOR PUBLIC WORKS AND PUBLIC SERVICES

Reports concerned with plans for public works contain a list of projects for the general improvement of the city and for its orderly growth. The emphasis is on physical development, which is important in creating a favorable climate for social and economic development. Programs for improving public services must be planned in the light of the physical, human, and financial resources of the community and its prospects for population and industrial growth. Three plans of this type are summarized below.

"Your Detroit"

This booklet was prepared by the Mayor's Postwar Improvement Committee of Detroit, Michigan.

The objectives of the public improvement program in Detroit are stated as follows:

1. To provide additional facilities designed to make our city a finer place in which to live and work.

2. To catch up on the needed public construction work which we postponed during the depression and the war.

3. To provide worthwhile employment for our returning servicemen and war workers during the period of industrial reconversion to peacetime production if necessary.

Among the projects planned and in various stages of completion are a new civic center; new express highways; widening, resurfacing, and straightening of existing streets; eliminating grade crossings; the construction of additional schools; more adequate recreational facilities; public housing construction; and new construction for public services.

The employment provided under this program is an incidental objective. The more important objectives are to bring the city's present facilities up to date and to construct new facilities in order to make Detroit a safer, happier, more comfortable community.

"Preliminary Ten-Year Post-War Capital Improvement Program"

This study was prepared by the planning director of the City Planning Board for consideration by the City Commission of Dayton, Ohio.

A ten-year program of capital investment is formulated on the assumption that the city can afford to spend a minimum of two and one-half million dollars a year for such improvements. The report lists various capital improvements according to the source or sources of revenue for financing them.

"Report to the People of Fort Lauderdale, Florida"

This report was issued by the Postwar Planning Committee of the Fort Lauderdale Chamber of Commerce. It consists of two parts: (1) a recommended public works program, and (2) recommendations for private enterprise to stimulate business, industry, and employment.

The public works program differs only in details, appropriate to the geographical setting of the city, from the Detroit and Dayton programs. Measures to stimulate business and employment include: (1) the continued development of Fort Lauderdale as a resort center, (2) the improvement of its services and commercial activities through better parking facilities, (3) the improvement of warehousing facilities, and (4) an increase in mass purchasing power by increasing the skills of people in the community.

COMPREHENSIVE CITY PLANNING

The first report below points out the important features in comprehensive planning. The second report is one of a series which makes up the master plan and emphasizes the important features in planning for the economic soundness and stability of a local area.

"Comprehensive City Plan: Greenville, Ohio"

The purpose of the Greenville study is "to serve as a guide in accomplishing the orderly, efficient, economical and attractive future development of Greenville—thereby to promote the health, safety, convenience, prosperity and welfare of its citizens, and to afford them a generally more satisfactory and satisfying community environment in which to live, work and play."

The methods used to achieve these purposes are both corrective and preventive. Corrective measures consist of a gradual and systematic carrying out of recommended improvements to remedy the present defects and deficiencies in the physical features of the community. Preventive measures, from the standpoint of physical development, refer to the passage and administration of a zoning ordinance, regulations controlling subdivisions, and a building code.

This plan is based on studies of the physical, social, and economic structure of the community. The following studies are examples:

1. Population studies. The study of the population growth, distribution, and age composition is essential to the city plan for these reasons:

    a. Community facilities (housing, recreation, parking areas, public buildings) should be planned according to population facts and trends.

    b. Comparison of the rate of growth with the rate for other cities, the county, the state, and the nation makes it possible to predict future population more accurately.

    c. Age composition of the community gives some indication of population increase. For example, the larger the proportion in the younger age group, the greater the natural increase in population. Greenville is seen as a comparatively mature community. A small proportion of young people indicates that its growth through natural increase will be small. The age composition is also important as an indicator of the kind of labor supply in the community.

2. The economic base. A study was made of the principal economic functions performed in the community. Any sound program for future development "must be in harmony with, and promotive of the major economic activities which furnish and will continue to furnish the livelihood of the people." A study of Greenville's economic structure, for example, reveals that it is primarily a trade and service center. Compared with a number of other cities in Ohio, it is much less industrialized. In view of this and in view of the further fact that Greenville has a good location with respect to markets, good transportation facilities, and a high grade of labor, the report concludes that the community could profitably expand industrially.

3. Land use. This is a survey of how the land is used in terms of the character, condition, height, size, and occupancy of all buildings and

structures, the characteristics of the space around them, and the location, extent, and condition of all public facilities and their uses. All parcels of land in the city and in the area within a half-mile of the corporate limits were investigated, and the data were recorded on large-scale maps. Various symbols and colors were used to differentiate the important features in connection with each piece of property. The land use maps give a comprehensive picture of many social and physical features about the community. Practically everything visible above the ground was portrayed on the maps. Such information is essential in pointing out deficiencies and in discovering corrective and preventive measures with regard to the development of the community.

A similar study and analysis was made of other important aspects of the community which affect the welfare of its residents: housing, zoning, subdivision control, thoroughfares, parking, public schools, parks and playgrounds, and public and semipublic buildings.

The plan of development outlined in the report is intended to serve the needs of Greenville for the next thirty years. The various projects in the plan are to be put into effect as the need arises and as funds ordinarily acquired for construction, repair, and improvements in the community become available.

"The Economy of the Cincinnati Metropolitan Area"

This report, one in a series that make up the master plan of development for the city and metropolitan area of Cincinnati, is the guide for their future economic development.

The first half of the report includes a brief description of the development of Cincinnati from a frontier village to a metropolis. A detailed analysis is made of the economy of this area as of 1940, followed by a study of the changes in the economy resulting from the war. Estimates are then made of the probable size and composition of the population in 1970. The last chapter, "Suggestions for Community Action," considers the objectives that are an outgrowth of the economic analysis and the means of achieving these objectives.

The second half of the report consists of appendices. In addition to statistical tables, the appendices include notes on the local tax structure, a method of measuring the seasonality of employment for various occupations, general and specific criteria for use in determining the suitability of occupations to the Cincinnati area, and the method used in making estimates of the future population and labor force.

EFFECTIVE COMMUNITY PLANNING

Since comprehensive planning is important from the standpoint of a community program to achieve stability of employment and a high level of employment, the question of what sound planning involves should be considered.

Two problems are involved: What are the prerequisites for the formulation and support of a community plan? What are the characteristics of a sound plan?

Foundations of a Sound Plan

Planning requires adequate financial support. It must have the participation of citizens. It must include the social and economic unit and not be limited to the political boundaries. Finally, local plans should be oriented with plans or developments in surrounding communities.

Financial Support. The planning activity should have some assurance of adequate financial support. Plans should be scaled to the ability of the taxpayer to support the projects included in the plan. This is especially important in the case of public works programs, since the cost of these programs must be borne in large measure by tax levies on the citizens in the community. In some cities where public funds are inadequate to provide for all needed improvements, supplementary funds have been subscribed by private organizations for general or for specific purposes.

Public Participation. Plans need moral as well as financial support from the people. Unless the majority of citizens in a community know enough about what is being planned to judge whether the planning is sound and in what way it promotes the public interest, the planning may be shaped in the interest of special groups. All means to keep the public informed should be utilized.

Support should be sought from public officials and community organizations. In the drawing of a master plan and in its realization, the participation of organizations such as the real estate board, the council of social agencies, the chamber of commerce, civic groups, and newspapers is desirable. Not only can these groups provide basic data about the community but also they may give technical assistance and assume responsibilities for promoting parts of the plan.

Planning for the Socio-economic Unit. Planning which stops at the city limits is unrealistic. The community will include, in many cases, the fringe area which surrounds the political boundaries of the city.

The problems of a city are also the problems of the area surrounding the city. Planning on a community-wide basis is one way of pointing out to rural and urban residents of the community their common interests and dependence on each other.

Coordination of Local Plans with Other Plans. The community plan should be coordinated with regional plans, state plans, and federal plans. Even though adjacent communities may have no plans, it is necessary to consider to some extent their history and their present social and economic structure, and to anticipate as well as possible how they are likely to develop in the future.

Characteristics of a Sound Plan

Community planning is sound if it is flexible, continuous, and comprehensive.

The first characteristic of a sound plan is flexibility. A plan is a blueprint which must be redrawn frequently in response to changing conditions. It is impossible to predict the order of importance of local problems five or ten years in the future. The future needs of communities are determined to a great extent by national policies and by a host of technological and social changes. Plans need periodic review and revision.

One rather common means of assuring flexibility in the planning procedure is to make broad plans for a six-year period, for example. At the end of each year the plans are carefully studied, and the program is revised in the light of conditions and prospects at that time. The plan is then extended to cover the next six-year period.

The second characteristic of a sound plan is continuity. One of the reasons why some excellent plans have not been successful is that no provision was made for continued interest in, and support of, the plans. Such a plan is simply shelved. Planning is a continuous process. The implementation of a plan may require ten, fifteen, twenty, or more years. This is one reason why the administration of local plans should be primarily the responsibility of local governments. Continuity in planning can thus be assured administratively, legally, and financially.

Patchwork or piecemeal plans too frequently pass for community planning. But, as pointed out by Walter Blucher, executive director of the American Society of Planning Officials, "a list of projects unrelated to the overall need (and) to the economic and social phases of the community does not constitute planning . . ."[1] A comprehensive

[1] American Society of Planning Officials, *News Letter,* No. 10 (May, 1944), 37-38.

plan sets down long-range policies and programs. It is more than a mere scheduling of programs which, taken individually, seem worthwhile. Some communities have obtained results with piecemeal plans, but too often the improvements have been temporary and have introduced elements of instability into the local economy, as in the case of communities which have sponsored an industrial expansion program without regard for other problems. A comprehensive plan not only covers all phases of community life, but it also recognizes interrelationships of each phase to the others. Programs of public works, or housing projects, or a program of industrial expansion are then planned in perspective.

REFERENCES

Aull, G. H. and J. M. Stepp. *The Postwar Economic Outlook in an Agricultural-Industrial Area.* Bulletin No. 355. Clemson: South Carolina Agricultural Experiment Station of Clemson Agricultural College, 1945. Pp. 43.

California State Reconstruction and Reemployment Commission. *Planning Pays Profits: The Story of San Diego.* Sacramento: The Commission, 1945. Pp. 32.

Chamber of Commerce of the United States. *A Procedure for Post-War Planning; Jobs and Production at War's End; Albert Lea, Minnesota, Charts a Course.* Washington: Chamber of Commerce of the United States, 1943. Pp. 59.

Chapin, F. Stuart, Jr. and Sam Schiller. *Communities for Living.* Athens: The University of Georgia Press, 1941. Pp. 56.

Cincinnati City Planning Commission. *The Economy of the Cincinnati Metropolitan Area.* Cincinnati: The Commission, 1946. Pp. 126.

Coates, Kenneth D., ed. *A City Looks at Itself.* Spartanburg, S. C.: Spartanburg Chamber of Commerce, 1945. Pp. 94.

Connecticut Public Expenditure Council, Inc. *Middletown, Testing Ground for Connecticut Postwar Planning.* Hartford: The Council, 1943. Pp. 32.

Dayton City Plan Board. *Preliminary Ten-Year Post-war Capital Improvement Program.* Dayton, Ohio: The Board, 1945. Pp.7.

Detroit, Michigan. Mayor's Post-war Improvement Committee. *Your Detroit.* Detroit: The Committee, 1944. Pp. 36.

Edwards, Allen D. *Population in Relation to Resources and Employment Opportunities in South Carolina.* Bulletin No. 358. Clemson: South Carolina Agricultural Experiment Station of Clemson Agricultural College, 1945. Pp. 62.

Fort Lauderdale Chamber of Commerce. *Report to the People of Fort Lauderdale, Florida.* Fort Lauderdale: Fort Lauderdale Chamber of Commerce, 1945. Pp. 39.

Greenville, Ohio, City Planning Commission. *Comprehensive City Plan.* Greenville: The Commission, 1945. Pp. 98. (Ladislas Segoe, Planning Consultant; Phillip L. Larson, Dale E. Lloyd, Cincinnati, Ohio.)

Kidner, Frank L. and Phillip Neff. *Los Angeles; The Economic Outlook.* Los Angeles: The Haynes Foundation, 1946. Pp. 25. (A condensation, prepared by Molly Lewin, of *An Economic Survey of Los Angeles* by the same authors.)

Louisville Area Development Association. *Action to Date.* Louisville, Ky.: The Association, 1945. Pp. 21.

New England Town Planning Association. *Community Planning for Younger Citizens; A Manual for Teachers.* Boston: The Association, n.d. Pp. 32.

San Diego Chamber of Commerce. *San Diego: As Others See Us!* San Diego, Calif.: San Diego Chamber of Commerce, 1945. Pp. 108.

Stonorov, Oscar and Louis I. Kahn. *You and Your Neighborhood.* New York: Revere Copper and Brass, Inc., 1944. 96 unnumbered pp.

Syracuse—Onondaga Post-War Planning Council. *The Post-War Report. 1945.* Syracuse, N. Y.: The Council, 1945. Pp. 154.

United States National Resources Committee, Regional Office, and New England Regional Planning Commission. *From the Ground Up.* Boston: The Committee, 1939. Pp. 54.

Virginia State Planning Board. *Preliminary Handbook on Local Planning.* Revised, November, 1943. Richmond: The Board, 1943. Pp. 38.

9

A Program for Community Action

A T THE NATIONAL LEVEL the Employment Act of 1946 asserts the responsibility of the national government for promoting full employment. At the local level there is no corresponding ordinance or charter amendment to assert the responsibility of the local community for promoting a high level of stable employment. Nevertheless, there are a number of communities which, through local initiative and effort, have taken measures to improve the soundness of their own economic structure.

The economic welfare of the city of Scranton, Pennsylvania, was threatened when the anthracite mines were exhausted. In 1942 a vigorous campaign to avert disaster was initiated by private interests and civic groups. As a result of the efforts of these groups sixty-three new industries were attracted to Scranton. The economic base of the city has been transformed.

The fishing season in Biloxi, Mississippi, begins in August and ends in April. The vacation season begins in April. Until recently, fishermen were unemployed from April to August, at the same time as hotel managers were looking for additional help. Stated in this way, the solution seems natural, but a dovetailing of industries took place only recently after study by a federal agency revealed a situation which had long existed in Biloxi. A solution might have been found earlier had the community through local effort taken stock of its problems and resources.

Other examples might be cited of ways in which local communities have achieved some measure of economic stability and have developed through a coordination of local efforts. Elyria, Ohio, has a stabilization bureau supported by firms which cooperate to stabilize employment. Each firm notifies the bureau of its needs and its anticipated layoffs. The labor supply is shifted from one industry to another. In Chicago a similar plan is in operation among six cooperating companies: a department store, a mail-order company, a candy

104

manufacturing establishment, two printing companies, and a food processing company.

No one group in the community is in position to accept the sole responsibility for achieving a high and stable level of economic activity. The problem is of vital interest to all groups. The preceding chapters have pointed out measures that may be considered independently by these groups. The purpose of this chapter is to outline a procedure for the coordination of these efforts in a community.

THE ORGANIZATION AND ACTIVITIES OF THE EMPLOYMENT COUNCIL

In order to coordinate the efforts of groups having a common interest in the community's economic development, it is suggested that an "Employment Council" be formed. The council will include representatives from industry, business, local government, labor, civic groups, planning groups, the newspapers, and radio. Ordinary citizens who are interested in the objectives of the organization should be invited to become members.

ORGANIZATION CHART

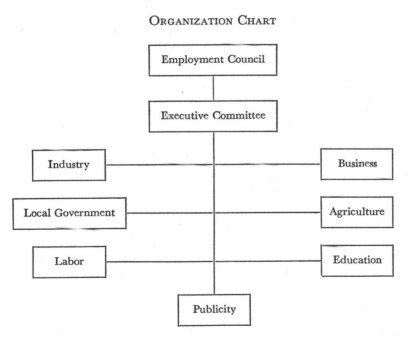

The chart reproduced above illustrates an organizational framework for the Employment Council, but the details will vary in each community. The Executive Committee will consist of elected officers and the chairmen of all working committees. The number of working committees will vary in different communities, with the seven working committees shown in the chart constituting a minimum. In some communities, subcommittees might be formed under the committees. For example, the committee on business might have subcommittees on financial institutions, retail trade, transportation, and resort trade.

The chairman of each working committee will be appointed by the chairman of the council. In turn, each working committee chairman will appoint members from among the organizations he represents to work with him.

Functions of the Council

A brief summary of the functions of such a council will be given in order to show in a more detailed and concrete manner the contribution which the council can make to the community. This will be followed by a description of the activities of each committee to show how the functions and purposes of the council may be implemented.

The objectives of the council are to coordinate the efforts of local groups interested in problems of full and stable employment, and to promote an action program based upon the economic needs and resources of the community.

In the achievement of these objectives the Employment Council will have the following functions:

1. Initiate surveys and make studies relating to employment and unemployment in the community.

2. Guide and assist committees in the technical phases of their work.

3. Coordinate the work of committees.

4. Determine economic objectives for the community.

5. Coordinate local plans with state and national plans.

6. Prepare an integrated plan of action showing the means by which local organizations can contribute to the common economic objectives.

7. Publicize the activities of the council; locally, as a means of getting continued support in the community; on a state and national basis, as a means of stimulating other communities.

Activities of the Working Committees

The work of each of the basic committees is described below. The report of each committee should include both the factual data gathered and its recommendations to the Employment Council. These recommendations will take the form of specific measures that have been tried out or that seem worth trying out. The Employment Council will then coordinate these proposals and submit a plan of action to be carried out in the community. At this stage the basic committees will assume the responsibility for making the proposals known to their respective groups or organizations and will assist them in carrying out proposals.

In order to illustrate the activities of each committee, some measures proposed in preceding chapters will be listed. A complete list should be made by each committee for its own use.

Committee on Industry. The following are primary activities of the Committee on Industry:

1. Survey the number and kinds of industries in the community.

2. Analyze the labor population in these industries by age, sex, color, occupation.

3. Secure statements from each firm on plans for contraction or expansion and the effect of these plans on labor needs.

4. Survey industrial sites: their size, location, cost, uses to which they may be put, proximity to transportation facilities, and other relevant information.

5. Survey past and present, active and inactive inquiries from industrial prospects and the nature of the responses by the local organizations receiving these inquiries.

6. Make a survey of employment stabilization plans, giving specific techniques used.

7. Make a study of natural resources in the community.

8. List the manufactured products which the community imports and exports.

The chairman of the committee will prepare a report for the Employment Council summarizing the findings of the committee, indicating the problems, and pointing out their significance in terms of the economic development of the community. The report to the Employment Council might include the following:

1. The nature and extent of local fluctuations in industrial employment.

2. A summary of the plans of local companies to raise or lower employment levels.

3. The experience of local companies with employment stabilization.

4. Recommendations regarding local use of employment stabilization methods.

5. The types of industrial expansion that should be encouraged in the community.

6. The presence or lack of suitable industrial sites.

Committee on Business. The Committee on Business will obtain essentially the same data from nonmanufacturing establishments in the community: wholesale and retail trade, service establishments, real estate, financial institutions, etc. Plans for employment stabilization are relatively less frequent in business than in industry. In some department stores, however, plans for stabilization of business have been put into effect. Business organizations are more directly concerned with stimulating trade and extending the trading area.

A survey of the trading area should be made and the resulting map included as part of the report. The reasons for the limits of the trading area should be investigated. Consideration should be given to the facilities, services, and events which will attract the farm population to trade in the community: roads, parking facilities, goods, and services needed by the farmer and provisions for recreation and participation in community life.

A study of products and services offered in the community may show that certain needs that could be met locally are being satisfied elsewhere or are not being satisfied at all.

These surveys and studies may result in such recommendations as these:

1. There is a local need for more restaurants and laundries. On the other hand, there are too many beauty shops in the community. Further expansion in this line should be discouraged.

2. Services of specialists such as market analysts, advertising specialists, and personnel technicians should be made available to small businesses on a cooperative basis. Such services will result in increased efficiency in the operation of small businesses.

3. Capital for new ventures, which require long-term loans and involve risks greater than those which an individual commercial bank can assume, should be made available through the creation of an equity bank.

4. A means should be found to enable small investors to share in the financing of new businesses.

5. The professional services of doctors, lawyers, dentists, and other specialists should be more readily accessible to the low and middle income groups. A small annual fee would insure this service. Under present circumstances a great part of the need for such services is not met.

6. Existing service occupations can stabilize and expand by providing additional related services.

Chapter 5 contains many other measures for achieving a balanced economic structure and for achieving stability of employment among business firms. The business committee must decide which ones are appropriate in a particular community.

Committee on Agriculture. The Committee on Agriculture will consist of a representative from a community farm organization who will serve as chairman, and committee members who are appointed by the chairman. This committee may include the following among its activities:

1. Make a survey of the kinds and quantities of agricultural products raised in the community annually.

2. Estimate how much of each product is marketed locally.

3. Make a study of products now imported into the community that could be grown profitably in the local area.

4. Find out what percentage of farm income is spent on various supplies, equipment, and services in the community.

5. Determine the adequacy of educational and vocational training facilities for the farm youth in the community.

6. In cooperation with the Committee on Business undertake a study of the methods for increasing the local demand for farm goods.

These studies may suggest some agricultural policies and measures that will promote the welfare of agriculture in the local and national economy and thereby contribute toward a program of full and stable employment. Proposals such as the following may be made:

1. Farmers working on land of low productivity should be encouraged to seek employment in expanding occupations.

2. Greater efficiency in farm operations will be attained if the results of research by federal and state agencies are used more widely. Agricultural agents, farm organizations, and agricultural schools must continue to educate farmers in these improved methods.

3. The risks involved in farming can be minimized by utilizing existing information about weather- and disease-resistant crops and breeds of livestock; by the use of insecticides, vaccines, and other preventive measures; and through crop selection and diversification.

4. The cooperative ownership of large farm equipment will give many of the advantages of mechanization and large-scale operation.

5. Cooperative buying and selling can be extended to include the buying of groceries, clothing, and furniture in addition to purchases of farm supplies and equipment.

6. Agriculture offers no opportunity for expansion in the total number of jobs available.

7. Urban and rural groups should try to find more industrial uses for farm products.

8. There may be a local need for storage and processing facilities.

Other measures are suggested in Chapter 6. Adaptations to meet local needs will result from the activities of the Committee on Agriculture.

Committee on Education. The school system influences the economic structure of the community in two important ways. First, it provides employment. Some of the ways in which the schools can promote stability of employment are described in Chapter 2.

In the second place, the kind of education and training provided by the school system determines to a considerable extent the kind of labor supply the community will have in the future. The following information would be of value in coordinating the interests, aptitudes, and training of students with community needs and opportunities:

1. A survey of the school population. This should include the number of boys and girls who each year enter junior and senior high school, drop out of school, or graduate. By plotting these data over a number of years, some estimates of the number of young people who will enter the labor market in future years may be made.

2. An analysis of business and vocational training offered in both public and private schools in the community.

3. Vocational interests of students in the junior and senior high schools.

4. Vocational guidance facilities provided in the community.

5. Extent and kind of in-service training provided to students in high schools and colleges in cooperation with businesses, industries, and local government.

6. The occupations of those entering the local labor market.

7. The extent of part-time and summer employment of high school and college students.

As a result of its activities the Committee on Education may make such recommendations as the following to the Employment Council:

1. A program of vocational guidance and training should be initiated in the senior high school.

2. A course on the history and present structure of the local economy should be made available to seniors in high school.

3. A cooperative work-study program should be provided for seniors in high school and postgraduate students.

Committee on Local Government. Local government influences the economic structure of the community in many ways. It hires people to provide public services; it encourages private business and industrial expansion; and by its purchasing policies it can support measures undertaken by industries to regularize their production schedules.

The following projects should be undertaken by a Committee on Local Government:

1. Survey of occupations and number of employees in public employment. This includes local employees of the city, county, state, and national governments.

2. Plans for public works in the community: kinds of projects, scheduling of projects, number of additional employees necessary to carry out these projects, and means of financing.

3. Specific techniques used by departments of local government to stabilize public employment.

4. Analysis of the cost per capita of various public services, and a comparison of what the tax dollar buys locally with what it buys in other cities of similar size in the state.

5. Statement of municipal indebtedness and methods of finance.

The Committee on Local Government may recommend such measures as the following to the Employment Council:

1. Adopt and enforce a zoning ordinance as a means of promoting social and economic stability in the local community.

2. Provide a continuous research program to determine the economic and social needs of the community and to provide the basis for planning the development of the community along sound lines.

3. Create a favorable climate for economic and social development through adequate provisions for recreation, parking facilities, transportation, power and light, the maintenance of health, and other services usually provided by municipalities.

4. Promote the development of housing to meet the needs of the lower income groups.

5. Administer the public works program so that it has, insofar as it can have, a contracyclical influence.

Committee on Labor. The Committee on Labor should include representatives from all national labor organizations operating in the community and from prominent independent unions. Any plans or measures affecting employment should be worked out in cooperation with this committee. Plans for vocational and apprenticeship training sponsored by schools should be coordinated with any similar service offered by unions. From the standpoint of the Employment Council the policies and practices of the unions, chiefly those policies which are directly related to employment opportunities and employment levels in the community, are matters of community interest.

While it is important to have organized labor represented on the Employment Council, in some cases it may not be desirable to have a separate labor committee. In Middletown, Connecticut, organized labor is represented on the Postwar Planning Council not as a separate labor committee but through membership in other committees. This arrangement was made at the request of members of organized labor.

Organized labor has a great stake in the economic well-being of the community. It also has responsibilities which must be recognized and accepted if a high standard of living and a high level of employment for workers are to be realized. The implications of this point of view have been discussed in Chapter 7. Among the points made in that chapter are the following:

1. Since the stability of labor policies and practices has an important effect on investment in new enterprises, labor organizations can encourage the increase in industrial employment by living up to both the spirit and the letter of the collective bargaining contracts which they accept.

2. Maintaining a company's competitive position is a means of keeping prices down and employment levels up. Feather-bedding or any other restrictive practice inevitably results in restriction of the national wealth and of the amount of goods and services available for distribution. For the nation as well as for any particular company, high prices reduce the amount of consumption, production, and employment.

3. Technological changes must be accepted. Organized labor can help to decrease the hardships of technological readjustment by promoting programs to retrain workers who are now in occupations which show declining opportunities.

4. Organized labor can actively support industrial and governmental security programs.

Committee on Publicity. The publicity committee will be responsible for informing community leaders and the public regarding the work of all committees of the Employment Council. The publicity program will be long-range, endeavoring to enlist and maintain popular support for the programs recommended.

Special Committees. The activities suggested for the various standing committees are concerned with determining community needs and problems and making plans to meet them. Additional information will be necessary. This can be obtained usually without a committee investigation. As an example, the total number employed and unemployed in the community may be obtained from the offices of the state employment service or the chamber of commerce. If these sources do not have the data, it may be necessary to assign the responsibility for securing this information to one or more of the committees or to appoint a special committee which will undertake that particular assignment.

No simple formula can be written by the Employment Council which will assure the achievement of its objectives. The work outlined for the committees is only preliminary to the more important job of stimulating and encouraging the adoption of measures, policies, and programs by employers and other groups in the community. Some of the measures and policies may have already been tried locally on a small scale; some of them may be new. All will have to be evaluated again. Each committee should continue to meet at regular intervals to study problems which arise. Progress reports should be submitted to the Employment Council periodically.

Employment Council and City Planning

The organization of the Employment Council has been described without indicating its relationship to a community planning commission. At the present time one-half of the cities in the United States having a population of 25,000 or more have official or unofficial public planning agencies. If a planning agency exists in the community, the Employment Council may function as a committee of the planning commission. Coordination between employment planning and other areas of planning is obviously important, since problems of employment bear some relationship to problems of housing, zoning, recreation, delinquency, health, and other factors that make the community desirable or undesirable as a place in which to live. In the absence of any community planning commission, an Employment Council should nevertheless be organized to serve its specific economic objectives. There is no single aspect of community life which is of greater importance to the community than its economic health. The Employment Council may provide the necessary impetus toward the creation of a planning commission by the public interest it arouses and by its achievements.

Organizing the Community for Action

A framework under which a community can work toward a high
level of stable employment has been presented. Emphasis is on local
responsibility for action and on the importance of coordinating the
efforts of existing local organizations in a concerted and sustained
approach to local problems. A community program for that purpose
has been outlined. How does one get the community started on such
a program of action? The following steps indicate the methods by
which an interested individual or group of individuals can proceed
in organizing the community for action.

Preparing an Initial Statement

The first step in organizing an Employment Council is the preparation of a concise and explicit statement giving the reasons for organizing a council and some illustrations of the results which it can
achieve. Examples of measures which can be adopted by local industries, business establishments, the local government, and other organized groups in an effort to achieve full and stable employment should
be specific and appropriate to the major types of businesses and industries in the community.

The material will describe the program to those persons who will
be asked to serve as sponsors and to the persons whom the sponsors
contact in an effort to organize the Employment Council.

Making Individual Contacts

The next step in the creation of an Employment Council is to make
individual contacts with a number of key persons in the community.
These key persons can serve two purposes: (1) to help in revising the
program for presentation to others, and (2) to promote the idea of a
council and a community program by becoming sponsors.

Meeting of Sponsors

A meeting of these key persons who have the time and the interest
to become sponsors of the program should be arranged. The general
purposes of this meeting will be to consider:

1. The recommendations or suggestions made by individual sponsors with regard to the statement outlining the program.

2. The method of getting the interest and support of the firms,
organized groups, and individuals that should be represented on the
Employment Council.

In connection with the second point, the sponsors will raise questions such as: What groups or individuals should become participants? Should each sponsor contact prospective members of the Employment Council individually or meet with them as a group? Should the program be confined to industries at the beginning and later extended to other organized segments of the community, or should the full council be organized at the start of the program? When, if at all, should the program receive publicity? How can necessary financial support be secured?

Forming the Nucleus of an Employment Council

If a full council is to be formed, the sponsors will contact the firms and organizations which should be represented on the council. The group forming the nucleus should include representatives from local government, the industries, business and trade organizations, labor organizations, farm groups, the schools, and the local employment office. If the sponsors decide to form an industrial committee first, only industrial establishments will be represented and a program for industry developed until such time as the sponsors and the industrial committee feel that the program should be broadened.

Finding the Key Man

The sponsors should find an enthusiastic, aggressive, and well-known leader in the community who will serve as a temporary chairman when a meeting is held to organize the Employment Council. It would normally be desirable to select someone from one of the industrial firms in the community, since the stability of employment in a community is probably affected to a greater degree by the policies and practices prevailing in industry than by those in any other field. The greatest need and opportunity for stabilizing employment is within industry. The key man should have prestige, enthusiasm, and qualities of leadership. The choice of a man to serve as temporary chairman should depend to a greater degree on these factors than on his affiliation with a particular group.

The First Meeting of the Employment Council

Interested individuals and representatives of agencies in the community should be called together by the temporary chairman. The meeting date should be set far enough in advance to avoid conflict with other meetings. Several steps can be taken at the first meeting:

1. Explanation of the reasons for organizing. This explanation

will be in rather general terms pending the outcome of the economic survey of the community. It should include a statement regarding the importance of coordinated local effort and public support in achieving full and stable employment.

2. The election of permanent officers: chairman, vice-chairman, secretary, and treasurer.

3. The appointment of a temporary planning committee made up of the elected officers and other members of the council appointed by the chairman in order to consider a method of completing the organization (committees, work of the committees, arranging meetings). This committee should meet before the second general meeting to consider such matters.

Completing the Organization

At the second meeting of members of the council, the temporary planning committee will present plans for a coordinated approach to problems of economic development. The business of this meeting will involve:

1. The appointment of committees to deal with all phases of economic life in the community. Each committee will consist of a chairman, who is a member of the Executive Committee (officers and chairman of each committee) and other members appointed by the chairman.

2. An explanation of the functions and duties of committees.

3. Scheduling the work of the committees.

4. An explanation of the purposes and methods of gathering factual information about the community.

5. A discussion of methods of financing the work of the council. Possible sources of funds include local companies, individuals, organizations, and government.

Creating a Fact-Finding Service

One of the first concrete steps which the Employment Council can take as soon as it is formed is the creation of a permanent fact-finding body. Neither the sponsors nor members of the council can be expected to carry on all the activities which are involved in a broad community program. A full-time paid staff, consisting of a director, secretary, and one or more research workers would serve the following functions:

1. Notify members of all meetings, keep minutes of the meetings, and in general keep a record of the activities of the council.

2. Upon the request of committee chairmen, or on its own initiative, gather and interpret facts which bear directly upon the work of the Employment Council.

3. Keep in touch with similar groups in other communities.

4. Make available in a central location any data and reports pertaining to the local community and other communities. This material will be available to members of local committees.

The director, on his own initiative or at the request of the council, may undertake additional activities. For example, if there is a need for more information about methods of stabilizing employment that have been tried and found successful, a lecture and discussion course can be organized. Another need that may become apparent is a better understanding of unemployment compensation laws. In states which have merit-rating provisions in the unemployment compensation act this is particularly important, since the employer's contribution rate can vary in some states from 1 to 4 per cent of his payroll, depending upon his experience in stabilizing employment.

Determining Economic Objectives for the Community

On the basis of the surveys and studies made by each committee, the Executive Committee will need to consider the specific economic objectives for the community. These will vary in each community depending upon its problems, its needs, and its resources.

A Program of Action

A program of community action should be prepared to meet the economic objectives. This will involve making specific recommendations to each of the organizations represented on the Employment Council. Farm organizations, industries, businesses, labor unions, and local government must be persuaded to modify their policies and practices to fit in with the community program.

Publicity

The program needs the interest and support of citizens of the community. A public works program, for example, needs community support, which may be stimulated by publicity concerning the order in which projects will be carried out, how they will be financed, when they will be completed, and their purpose and place in the community program. The program of the council should, therefore, be made known to citizens of the community through radio broadcasts, newspaper stories, and public meetings.

Follow-up

Any program of action will need to be reviewed periodically and modified. Some problems in the implementation of a program cannot be anticipated. The Executive Committee should meet at regular intervals to report on the progress being made by each committee and to meet problems as they arise. The program of action needs continuity and flexibility.

CONCLUSION

This procedure for organizing the community is suggestive rather than definitive or rigid. Local differences—in problems, in the economic structure, in the interests of citizens—will necessitate modifications in the suggested procedure. The leaders in each community can best determine the specific procedure to follow in stimulating the interest and the support of citizens and organized groups.

Each community will be affected by the general economic conditions of the country; but each community will also determine to some degree what the general economic condition of the nation will be. Local resourcefulness and local effort will, therefore, not only affect the stability and the level of employment in the particular community but will also have effects which extend beyond the community.

REFERENCES

Black, Russell Van Nest, and M. H. Black. *Planning for the Small American City; An Outline of Principles and Procedure Especially Applicable to the City of Fifty Thousand or Less.* No. 87. Chicago: Public Administration Service, 1944. Pp. 86.

Chamber of Commerce of the United States. *A Procedure for Post-War Planning; Jobs and Production at War's End; Albert Lea, Minnesota, Charts a Course.* Washington: Chamber of Commerce of the United States, 1943. Pp. 59.

Colcord, Joanna C. *Your Community; Its Provision for Health, Education, Safety, and Welfare.* New York: Russell Sage Foundation, 1947. Pp. 263.

Committee for Economic Development. *Handbook for Community Fact-Finding and Local Research Division.* New York: The Committee, 1944. 12 unnumbered pp.

——. *Jobs in Your Town—After the War.* New York: The Committee, 1944. Pp. 51.

——. Agricultural Communities Committee. *Postwar Jobs and Growth in Small Communities.* New York: The Committee, 1944. Pp. 16.

Connecticut Public Expenditure Council, Inc. *Middletown, Testing Ground for Connecticut Postwar Planning.* Hartford: The Council, 1944. Pp. 32.

Field, Arthur M. *Outline for a Community Industrial Development Program.* Charleston, S. C.: The American Industrial Development Council, 1946. Pp. 76.

Lohmann, Karl B. *Principles of City Planning.* New York: McGraw-Hill Book Co., 1931. Pp. 395.

Morrow, Cornelius Earl. *Planning Your Community; A Manual of Suggestions for Practical Community Planning.* New York: Regional Plan Association, 1945. Pp. 42.

Public Administration Service. *Action for Cities; A Guide for Community Planning.* No. 86. Chicago: The Service, 1945. Pp. 77.

Segoe, Ladislas et al. *Local Planning Administration.* Chicago: International City Managers' Association, 1941. Pp. 699.

United States Bureau of Foreign and Domestic Commerce. *Community Action for Post-War Jobs and Profits.* Industrial Series No. 6. Washington: Government Printing Office, 1943. Pp. 39.

——. *Small Town Manual for Community Action!* Industrial Series No. 4. Washington: Government Printing Office, 1942. Pp. 46.

United States National Resources Committee, Regional Office, and New England Regional Planning Commission. *From the Ground Up.* Boston: The Committee, 1939. Pp. 54.